COMPLETE GUIDE TO INDIAN COOKING AND ENTERTAINING

From Mom with Love ..

PUSHPA BHARGAVA

For more information, address: info@momsindiancooking.com or www.momsindiancooking.com

The Front Cover: The background is an environmentally friendly jute bag (called "bora" in Hindi) used for centuries in India for transporting and storing cereals and spices in large quantities. The bottom right is the traditional "Masal Dan" (spice container) - a must in every Indian kitchen. The everyday spices are (clockwise from the one o' clock position): Dry Mango Powder, Cumin Seeds, Mustard Seeds, Turmeric Powder, Red Chili Powder, Coriander Powder, and Salt in the middle.
Photo: Anjali Bhargava, www.anjalibhargava.com
Original Design: Shyamlee Malhotra

Published by: Crest Books, Inc. 19 Dorfer Lane, Nesconset, NY 11767, USA

Printed at: Thomson Press (India) Limited.

Library of Congress Control Number: 2008912013
ISBN: 978-0-9761851-2-3

First Edition March 2007
Second Edition March 2009
Third Printing July 2010

Price: US $ 27.95
       Canada $ 33.95

$27.95
ISBN 978-0-9761851-2-3
52795>

9 780976 185123

Dedicated to my mother
who taught me everything I know about cooking.
Also to my children,
and my grandchild, Eesha
who will hopefully use this book
to prepare meals for their loved ones

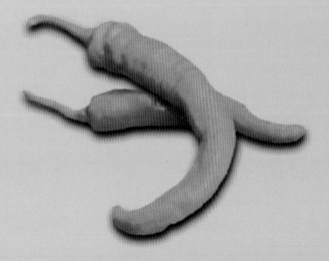

CONTENTS

(v) Vegan or Vegan Option

(v) Vegan or Vegan Option

(v) Vegan or Vegan Option

ACKNOWLEDGEMENTS

Where do I begin?

My mom - the very best cook in the world - who always left a little dough at the end of her cooking and patiently guided my tiny hands as I tried to roll out the last few "rotis."

My mother-in-law who, in spite of having a very busy political career, always found a little time to prepare a special treat for her children.

Usha Bhabhi for coming up with the idea of writing this book and her constant encouragement and guidance.

Aruna Bhabhi for her literary guidance and sharing her special recipes.

Urmil Handa for sharing her recipes.

Dawn Joseph for her loving work on the typing of the manuscript.

Bina and Gurdial Singh for their invaluable help in the editing and printing of this book.

Anita and Pravin Mehta for the very personal interest they have taken in this book.

Vandana, Anjali, Gauri and Shyamlee for the loving work on the design, photography and creative suggestions.

My children Vivek, Vibha, Vandana and Vivek for being just that - loving children - and their help and constant inspiration.

Last but not least, my husband and best friend, Vikram, for his constant support and work on the book throughout the whole process.

READ THIS FIRST....

- Please make sure you look at the preparation and cooking time in advance of a meal or party. While some recipes take only a few minutes, others may need preparation days in advance.

- Likewise, please make sure you have the proper kitchenware for the recipe you are using. As an example, you really can not make good idlis without an idli maker.

- It is a good idea to make and freeze ingredients ahead of time. This way you can prepare meals that would take days or hours in a matter of minutes. Some examples are precooked masala and chutneys.

- I have tried to provide optimum amounts of salt, cooking time, water to be added, etc. to save you a lot of trial and error. However, please be aware that slight variations may occur from kitchen to kitchen in water absorption of different brands of flour, due to altitude, etc. Most importantly, individual tastes for salt, spice and sugar vary. Some adjustments to the recipes may be needed based on the above. For a really important meal, a "trial run" may be a good idea.

- ! Caution: Use extreme care when deep frying. Due to a combination of factors, the object being fried may burst causing the hot oil to spatter. Some of the causes can be adding too much water, the oil being too hot, or the ingredients being old stock due to poor turnover in the store. It is always advisable to stand a fair distance away from the stove until you have made sure this is not happening. Also, you can hold a spatter screen as a safe guard.

- For a hassle free cooking experience pre-measure all the ingredients in small bowls and arrange in the order of use before starting to cook. See picture below.

- Vegan (or Vegan option) dishes are marked with a (v) in the Contents.
- For difficult to follow instructions such as rolling dough, please be sure to take advantage of:

Website: www.momsindiancooking.com

PREFACE TO SECOND EDITION

I am truly touched by the overwhelming response to the first edition of the book.

I have made a few minor modifications to some of the recipes based on the user feedback and have added some recipes based on popular requests. I hope the readers find the second edition even more useful than the first one.

Pushpa Bhargava

INTRODUCTION

If you were to own just one book of Indian cuisine, this is it. It is a complete guide to Indian cooking. It is a substitute for your Mom standing next to you and lovingly helping you prepare excellent, nutritious Indian meals for every occasion.

If you want to cook Indian food but do not know what spices, legumes, beans, and pots and pans you need - you don't have to worry - a complete pantry list is provided. There is a pantry list for beginners and another one for more committed and experienced cooks - all in a convenient format that you can take right to the store with you.

With this book in your kitchen, whether you are having a party or preparing a quiet meal for your family, you don't have to go through different cook books to come up with a menu. It is all here – a complete list of menu combinations for different occasions both special and everyday.

This book will provide you with solutions for all your cooking, entertaining, and household needs:
- Ideas about foods you can cook and freeze ahead of time for occasions when you need to produce a meal in a hurry or are just too tired to cook.
- Suggestions on how to deal with cooking crises such as a sauce that has become too watery or a dish that is too salty.
- Tips for storing and preparing precooked masalas and efficient ways to freeze chutneys.
- Safety tips such as how to quickly put out a minor fire on your stove.
- Guidelines for cleaning and odor removal.
- Home remedies for minor ailments such as cough and colds, upset stomachs and abdominal colic pains that babies often suffer from.
- Lots of demos and useful information at www. momsindiancooking.com

The most special and unique feature of this book is the TLC tips. These are little short cuts and little secrets that will make your cooking easier, yet delicious.

This book is a must have for every kitchen. It is an invaluable gift to give to anyone who loves to cook or would like to try. It is truly a garland of rare gems collected over a lifetime of experience and given to you as a special gift.

From Mom with love!

Glossary of Common Hindi Words

HINDI NAME	ENGLISH NAME	PICTURE ON PAGE
Achar	Pickle (condiment)	
Adrak	Ginger	
Ajwain	Lovage, carom seeds	10
Alu	Potato	
Am	Mango	
Amchur/Khatai	Dried mango powder	10
Anannas	Pineapple	
Anar Dana	Dried pomegranate seed	10,173
Angoor	Grapes	
Arhar Dal	A variety of lentils	10
Atta	Whole wheat flour	
Badam	Almonds	
Badi Elaichi	Black cardamom	10
Baghar	Tempering	10
Baigan	Eggplant	
Belan	Rolling pin	9
Besan	Gram flour	
Bhaji/Subzi	Cooked vegetable	
Bhindi	Okra	
Bhuna Jeera	Roasted cumin seeds	173
Chai	Tea	
Chakla	Circular piece of board on which dough is rolled	
Chana Dal	Shelled split gram seeds	10
Chapati	Unlevened whole wheat bread	103
Chawal	Rice (Basmati is the preferred type, others are Patna, long grain, Texmati, etc.)	
Chimta	Tongs	
Chhilka Mung Dal	Split unshelled mung beans	10
Chini	Sugar	
Chhole	Chickpeas	10
Chhonk Ka Bartan	Small frying pan for tempering	10
Chhonk	Tempering	10
Chutney	Tangy Indian Relish	140
Curry Patta	Curry leaf - aromatic leaves used mostly for south Indian cooking	
Dahi	Yogurt	170
Dalchini	Cinnamon	

HINDI NAME	ENGLISH NAME	PICTURE ON PAGE
Dhania	Coriander	
Dhokla Maker	Stand with containers for steaming dhokla	9
Dhuli Mung Dal	Shelled, split and washed mung beans	10
Doodh	Milk	
Elaichi	Green cardamom	10
Gajar	Carrot	
Garam Masala	Blend of Indian spices (includes cumin, pepper, cardamom, etc.)	
Ghee	Clarified butter	169
Gud/Gur	Jaggery	
Gulab Jal	Rose Essence	9
Haldi	Turmeric	10
Hara Dhania	Green coriander leaves (also called cilantro)	
Hari Mirch	Green chili pepper	
Hing	Asafetida	10
Idli Maker	Stand with containers to steam Idli	9
Imli	Tamarind	
Imli Paste	Tamarind paste	
Jaiphal	Nutmeg	
Javitri	Mace	
Jeera	Cumin seed	10
Jharar	Slotted spoon/skimmer	9
Jhinga	Prawn/shrimp	
Kaju	Cashew nuts	
Kala Namak	Black salt	10
Kalaunji	Onion seeds	10
Kali Mirch	Peppercorn	10
Karchhi	Ladle	
Kadhai	Cast iron wok	9
Kathal	Jackfruit	
Kela	Banana	
Kesar	Saffron	10
Kewra	Kewra Flower Essence	9
Khas Khas	Poppy seeds	
Khatai/Amchur	Dried mango powder	10
Kheera	Cucumber	

HINDI NAME	ENGLISH NAME	PICTURE ON PAGE
Khumbh	Mushroom	
Kishmish	Raisins	
Lahsan	Garlic	
Lal Mirchi (Pisi)	Red chili powder	10
Lal Mirchi (Sabut)	Red whole chili	10
Laung	Cloves	10
Macchi	Fish	
Maida	All purpose flour	
Makki Atta	Corn flour	
Malai	Cream	
Mamra/Murmure	Puffed Rice	
Masal Dan	Spice box (circular steel container with 6-7small containers inside)	10
Masoor Dal	Shelled red lentils	10
Matar	Peas	
Mauth	A smaller variety of pulse similar to mung beans	10
Meetha Neem	Aromatic leaves used mostly for South Indian cooking	
Methi Dana	Fenugreek seeds	10
Methi Patta	Fenugreek leaves	
Mirch	Chili pepper	
Mung Dal (Chhilka)	Unshelled split mung beans	10
Murgh	Chicken	
Murmure/Mamra	Puffed Rice	
Namak	Salt	10
Nan	All purpose leavened bread traditionally baked in tandoor	94
Nariyal	Coconut	
Nimbu	Lemon	
Palak	Spinach	
Panchmel Dal	Five dals (arhar, chana, masoor, mung and urad)	
Paneer	Home made Indian cheese	171
Pao	Bun	35
Papad/Papadum	Thin spiced wafers usually made with urad or mung dal	
Parantha	Shallow fried whole wheat flat bread	103
Patta Gobhi	Cabbage	
Phool Gobhi	Cauliflower	
Pishta	Pistachio	

HINDI NAME	ENGLISH NAME	PICTURE ON PAGE
Podina	Mint leaves	
Pohe	Flattened/pounded rice	
Poori	Deep fried unleavened whole wheat bread	104
Pyaz	Onion	
Rai	Mustard seeds	10
Raita	Spicy yogurt (with vegetables)	143
Rajma	Kidney beans	62
Roti	Unleavened whole wheat bread	105
Sag	Green leafy vegetable	
Sabji/Subzi	Cooked vegetable	
Saboodana	Tapioca	10
Sabut Masoor	Whole lentils	10
Sabut Urad	Whole urad	10
Sarson	Mustard leaves	64
Saunf	Fennel seeds	10
Saunth	Ginger powder	10
Sev	Apple	
Sev	Savory snack	
Sevain	Vermicelli (Indian Style)	159
Shakkar/Chini	Sugar	
Simla Mirch	Bell pepper/capsicum	
Sooji	Semolina	
Tadka	Tempering	10
Tamatar	Tomato	
Tandoor	Clay oven	
Tartri	Citric acid	
Tawa	Shallow cast iron pan for making roti	9
Tej Patta	Bay leaves	10
Thali	High lipped steel plate	10
Til	Sesame seeds	
Toor Dal/Arhar Dal	A variety of lentils	10
Tulsi	Green aromatic leaves in basil family	
Urad Dal	A variety of whitish yellow dal	10
Wark/Warak	Silver foil	

1. Roti Station (Tawa, cake rack and rolling pin)
2. Slotted Spoon (Jharar) and Kadhai
3. Idli and Dhokla Maker (left)
4. Typical Pantry for Indian Cooking
5. Dry Measure
6. Kewra and Rose Essence

1. Bay Leaves
2. Flattened Rice
3. Fennel Seeds
4. Black Cardamom
5. Cinamon Sticks
6. Semolina
7. Coriander Seeds
8. Peppercorn
9. Green Cardamom
10. Tapioca
11. Dry Red Chilies

12. Fenugreek Seeds
13. Black Salt
14. Ground Pomegranate Seeds
15. Saffron
16. Ground Asafetida
17. Onion Seeds
18. Cloves
19. Carom Seeds
20. Roasted, Ground Cumin
21. Ginger Powder (around center)

1. Chick Peas
2. Whole Lentils
3. Toor/Arhar
4. Unshelled Split Mung
5. Whole Urad
6. Washed Lentils
7. Washed Urad Dal
8. Kidney Beans
9. Black Gram
10. Gram Dal
11. Whole Mung
12. Mauth
13. Washed Mung

Pakodi drop/fry

Masal Dan
1. Salt
2. Mustard Seeds
3. Turmeric Powder
4. Coriander Powder
5. Red Chili Powder
6. Dried Mango Powder
7. Cumin Seeds

Tempering

THE PANTRY – EVERYDAY ESSENTIALS CHECKLIST

Every Day Cooking
in 'Masal Dan'

- ❑ Salt
- ❑ Red Chili Powder
- ❑ Cumin Seeds
- ❑ Coriander Powder
- ❑ Amchur Powder
- ❑ Turmeric Powder
- ❑ Mustard Seeds
- ❑ Asafetida

Occasional Masaala
in Small Glass Jars

- ❑ Chana Masala
- ❑ Garam Masala
- ❑ Roasted Cumin Powder
- ❑ Bay Leaves
- ❑ Black Cardamom
- ❑ Peppercorn
- ❑ Cloves
- ❑ Green Cardamom
- ❑ Cinnamon Sticks
- ❑ Ground Black Pepper

Cooking Flour and Grains
in Cans or Plastic Containers

- ❑ Basmati Rice
- ❑ Whole Wheat Flour

Hot Drinks & Baking Needs
Fancy Containers on the Counter

- ❑ Coffee
- ❑ Tea Bags
- ❑ Sugar

In the Pantry
in Large Glass Jars

- ❑ Arhar Dal
- ❑ Urad Dal
- ❑ Mung Dal

Canned Goods

- ❑ Red kidney Beans
- ❑ Chickpeas
- ❑ Tomato Puree

Special Kitchenware

- ❑ Medium Kadhai
- ❑ Small Pan for Tempering
- ❑ Coffee Grinder
- ❑ Blender
- ❑ Egg Beater
- ❑ Pressure Cooker
- ❑ Jharar (Slotted Spoon)
- ❑ Tawa
- ❑ Rolling Pin
- ❑ Cake Rack for Rotis
- ❑ Tongs

In the Refrigerator

- ❑ Jams
- ❑ Eggs
- ❑ Syrup
- ❑ Ketchup
- ❑ Butter
- ❑ Milk
- ❑ Juices
- ❑ Bread
- ❑ Bottled Lemon Juice
- ❑ Yogurt

In the Freezer

- ❑ Peas
- ❑ Corn
- ❑ Pre Cooked Masala
- ❑ Frozen Rotis

Vegetables

- ❑ Potatoes
- ❑ Onions

Oils

- ❑ Cooking Oil
- ❑ Ghee

Dry Goods

- ❑ Paper Towels
- ❑ Napkins

THE COMPLETE PANTRY

Every Day Cooking:
(In the 'Masal Dan')
Coriander Powder
Cumin Seeds
Dry Mango Powder
Mustard Seeds
Red Chili Powder
Salt
Turmeric Powder

Occasional Masala and Other Cooking Ingredients:
(In Small Glass Jars)
Amti Powder
Asafetida
Baking Powder
Baking Soda
Bay Leaves
Biryani Masala
Black Cardamom
Black Salt
Chat Masala
Cinnamon Sticks
Citric Acid
Cloves
Dried Coconut Powder
Eno's Fruit Salt
Fennel Seeds
Garam Masala
Ginger Powder
Green Cardamom
Ground Black Pepper
Honey
Kebab Masala
Kewra Essence
Mace
Nutmeg
Pani Poori Masala
Pao Bhaji Masala
Paprika
Peppercorn
Pomegranate Seeds
Powder Milk
Raisins
Roasted Cumin Powder
Rose Essence
Saffron

Sambhar Powder
Tandoori Masala
Whole Red Chili

Cooking Flour and Grains:
(In Cans or Plastic Containers)
All Purpose Flour
Basmati Rice
Corn Flour
Flattened Rice (Pohe)
Gram Flour
Long Grain Rice
Semolina
Whole Wheat Flour

On the Counter:
(Fancy Containers)
Coffee
Sugar
Tea Bags

Dals and Others:
(In Large Glass Jars)
Arhar Dal
Black Gram
Chickpeas
Mauth
Mung Dal
Red Kidney Beans
Red Lentils
Split Unshelled Mung Dal
Tapioca
Urad Dal
Whole Lentils
Whole Mung
Whole Urad

Cold Drinks:
Juice
Soda

Canned Goods:
Chickpeas
Crushed Tomatoes
Fruits
Mango Pulp
Other Canned Vegetables such as Jack Fruit

Red Kidney Beans
Tomato Paste
Tomato Puree

Miscellaneous:
Papad
Pickles

In the Refrigerator:
Bottled Lemon Juice
Bread
Butter
Coriander Leaves
Eggs
Fruits
Garlic
Ginger
Green Chili
Jams
Juices
Ketchup
Lemon
Milk
Salad Vegetables
Syrup
Tamarind Paste

Frozen Food:
Pre Cooked Masala
Corn
Frozen Rotis
Fruits
Mixed Vegetables
Okra
Paneer
Peas
Spinach

Vegetables Outside the Refrigerator :
Onions
Potatoes

Nuts:
Almonds
Cashew Nuts
Peanuts
Pistachios
Walnuts

Snacks:
Chips
Cookies
Dehydrated Fruits
Indian Salty Snacks
Mathri
Salsa

Breakfast:
Breakfast Cereals

Oils:
Cooking Oil
Ghee
Mustard Oil

Dry Goods:
Cold Cups
Hot Cups
Napkins
Paper Plates
Paper Towels
Plastic Spoons, Forks,
Knives

Routine Implements:
Blender
Coffee Grinder
Egg Beater
Food Processor
Grater

Special Kitchenware and Implements:
Cake Rack for Rotis
Cheesecloth
Large Strainer
Medium Kadhai
Pressure Cooker
Rolling Pin
Slotted Spoon (Jharar)
Small Kadhai
Small Pan for Tempering
Tawa
Tongs

WEIGHTS, MEASURES AND TEMPERATURE CONVERSION CHART

Temperature

$$^{0}C = (Deg\ F-32)x\ ^{5}/_{9}$$
$$^{0}F = (Deg\ C)x\ ^{9}/_{5} +32$$

Degrees F	Rounded ^{0}C
475	250
450	230
425	220
400	200
375	190
350	175
325	160
300	150
275	135
250	120

For example:
$$212\ ^{0}F = (212-32)x\ ^{5}/_{9} = 100\ ^{0}C$$
$$100\ ^{0}C = 100\ x\ ^{9}/_{5}+32 = 212\ ^{0}F$$

Weights

1 oz = 1/16 lb

1 lb = 454 gm

Ounce (oz)	Grams (gm) (rounded)
$^{1}/_{2}$	15
1	30
2	60
3	85
4	115
8 ($^{1}/_{2}$ lb)	230
12	340
16 (1 lb)	455

Volume (US Measure)

1 ounce = 1/128

gallon = 29.57 ml

US Ounce (oz)	Milliliter (ml) (rounded)
$^{1}/_{2}$	15
1	30
2	60
4	120
8	240
12	355
16	475
64 ($^{1}/_{2}$ gallon)	1,895
128 (1 gallon)	3,785

TLC Tip: *Please note that measuring cups are different for dry and liquid ingredients. Use cups specifically intended for dry and liquid measures, and measuring spoons for measuring teaspoon and tablespoon.*

SAMPLE MENU COMBINATIONS

MEAL TYPE	COMBINATION 1	COMBINATION 2	COMBINATION 3
Party Appetizers	Dhokla Dhania and Podina Chutney	Vegetable Pakoda Imli Chutney	Vegetables and Dip Mixed Nuts
Party Meal	Matar Paneer Gobhi Alu Kadhai Chicken Boondi Raita Salad Tandoori Roti Rice Mango Ice Cream Tea/Coffee	Dal Makhani Bhindi Masala Sag Paneer Rogan Josh Cucumber Raita Onion and Tomato Salad Nan Rice Kheer Tea/Coffee	Dum Alu Baigan Bharta Besan ki Mirch Rajasthani Chicken Dahi Baday Salad Nan Rice Rasgulla Tea/Coffee
Brunch	Idli Sambhar Nariyal Chutney Dahi Bhat Sevain Kheer	Poori Chatpate Alu Anannas Lonji Amras	Alu Parantha Plain Yogurt (with salt, roasted cumin and red chili powder) Sukhi Matar Gulab Jamun
Lunch with Company	Chhole Bhature Dahi Baday Sooji Halwa	Pulao Papri Chat Achar Papad Fruit Cream	Chicken Biryani Palak Raita Srikhand
Everyday Evening Meal	Arhar Dal Sukhe Alu Salad Roti Rice Mint Chutney	Urad Dal Bhindi Masala Salad Roti Dhania and Podina Chutney	Dahi ke Alu Karela Parantha Salad
Chat	Pani Poori Alu Tikki Besan Burfi Mango Lassi	Papri Chat Dhokla Mango Ice Cream Lassi	Bhel Poori Pao Bhaji Ras Malai Mango Lassi

Breakfast & Brunch Dishes

Ande Ki Bhurji or Masala Omelet

Spicy Scrambled Eggs

Serves 4

Preparation time: 30 mins.
Cooking time: 15 mins.

Ingredients:

8 large eggs
2 tablespoons oil
$^1/_2$ teaspoon cumin seeds (optional)
1 large onion, chopped
1 green chili, finely chopped
2 medium tomatoes, diced (optional)
1 teaspoon salt
$^1/_4$ teaspoon red chili powder
$^1/_2$ teaspoon garam masala
2 tablespoons coriander, finely chopped

Method:

Beat eggs until frothy.
Heat oil in pan on medium heat. Add onions and green chilies. Stir until onions are soft. Add tomatoes and sauté (optional). While the onions and tomatoes are cooking, beat eggs again and add all the ingredients except cumin Add egg mixture to pan and stir until cooked to taste.
Optional: Add cumin seeds to hot oil. Stir until light brown and follow the above.
For masala omelet, add all of the above ingredients except oil and tomatoes to the frothy egg mixture.

Serving suggestion
Serve with bagels or toast, accompanied with fruit juice, fruit, coffee, or masala chai. Makes a sumptuous brunch.

Preferred kitchenware
• *Large nonstick frying pan*
• *Medium size mixing bowl*

Idli
Popular South Indian Steamed Rice Cake

Serves 4

Preparation time: Overnight
Cooking time: 15 mins. per batch

🍎 *TLC Tip: Preparation for idlis start a day before you plan to serve. Soak the following* in separate bowls. You should have an idli maker before you start!*

Ingredients:
*1 cup urad dal
*2 cups rice
$1^1/_4$ cups water (for grinding dal)
1 cup water (for grinding rice)
1 teaspoon salt
1 teaspoon cumin seeds (optional)
4 cups water (for steaming)

Method:
Soak dal and rice in separate bowls for 8-10 hours, one day before. Drain and grind dal and rice separately in blender, adding water as needed. The consistency should be that of pancake batter. Combine and stir to mix well. Store overnight in large bowl with lid in a warm place.
🍎 *TLC Tip: Place in oven with the light on.*
Next morning, the batter should rise to about twice its original volume. Stir well and add 1 teaspoon salt and 1 teaspoon cumin seeds (optional). Mix.
Place idli maker in large saucepan. Add 4 cups of water (the water should not reach the idli maker

Serving suggestion
Serve with piping hot sambhar and coffee or masala chai.

Preferred kitchenware
- *2 Medium bowls for soaking dal and rice*
- *Large mixing bowl with lid*
- *Blender*
- *8 qt. saucepan with lid*
- *Idli maker*
- *Butter knife*

molds). Grease idli molds and pour about 2 tablespoons of batter in each section. Stack moulds one on top of the other. Cover. Place saucepan on stove on high heat and turn to medium when water starts to boil. Steam for about 12 minutes. Remove idli maker from saucepan, separate the trays and allow them to cool for 5 minutes. Remove idlis using butter knife and place in a serving bowl. Repeat procedure for the remaining batter.

❦ *TLC Tip: The following is a great recipe for leftover idlis: Slice idlis horizontally. In a frying pan add 1 tablespoon of oil. When oil is hot, add $\frac{1}{4}$ teaspoon of mustard seeds. Wait till they start to pop. Place sliced idlis in pan. Sprinkle salt on them. When idlis turn crisp, golden brown, turn them over. They are delicious with butter or chutney.*

Short cut recipe for idlis:

Ingredients:
1 cup urad dal flour
2 cups rice flour
1 teaspoon Eno fruit salt*

Mix the 2 flours with water to the consistency of pancake batter. Cover and store in warm place overnight. Just before making idlis, add Eno fruit salt.
Follow instructions above for steaming idlis.

*Available in Indian grocery stores

Pohe
Flattened Rice
Serves 4

Preparation time: 15 mins.
Cooking time: 15 mins.

Ingredients:
2 cups flattened rice*
4 tablespoons oil
$^1/_2$ teaspoon mustard seeds
5-6 curry leaves (karhi patta)
1 small green chili, chopped
1 small onion, finely chopped
$^1/_4$ teaspoon turmeric powder
$^1/_2$ teaspoon salt
1 small potato, boiled and cut into cubes
$^1/_4$ cup peas, shelled or thawed if frozen
2 tablespoons lemon juice
$^1/_4$ teaspoon red chili powder
2 tablespoons coriander, chopped

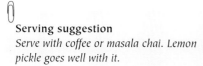

Serving suggestion
*Serve with coffee or masala chai. Lemon
pickle goes well with it.*

Preferred kitchenware
• *Large nonstick frying pan with lid*
• *Large strainer*

Method:
Put flattened rice in strainer and wash under running water until it is soaked (do not over soak). Leave in strainer for draining for 10 minutes. Heat oil in frying pan on medium-high heat. Add mustard seeds and curry leaves and green chili. When seeds start to pop, add onions, turmeric powder, salt, potatoes and peas. Cover and cook for 3 minutes (so potatoes are soft but not browned). Add flattened rice, cook for 2 to 3 minutes, stirring occasionally (taking care not to break grains). Add lemon juice and red chili powder. Cover and reduce to low heat for 2 to 3 minutes. Turn off stove and leave frying pan covered for another 5 minutes. Garnish with chopped coriander.

*Flattened rice is available at Indian grocery stores

Chhunke Mung or Chana or Mauth

Sprouted Mung Beans, Black Gram or Mauth*

Serves 4

Preparation time: 3 days
Cooking time: 5-10 mins.

Ingredients:

1 cup whole mung (or black gram or mauth)
1 tablespoon oil
Pinch of asafetida
$1/_8$ teaspoon turmeric powder
$1/_4$ teaspoon salt
$1/_4$ cup water
$1/_4$ teaspoon red chili powder
2 tablespoons coriander, chopped
1 fresh lemon, cut in quarters
1 medium tomato, chopped

Method:

Wash and soak mung beans overnight in bowl.
🌿 *TLC Tip: Sometimes there are small pieces of rock, foreign matter, etc. in the mung beans. Be sure to pick these out.*
Drain and cover for 24 hours until mung beans have sprouted. Remove grains of mung that have not sprouted and are still hard.
Heat oil in pan on medium-high heat. Add asafetida, turmeric powder, sprouted mung, salt and water. Stir and cover. Reduce heat to medium-low. Cook for 5 to 6 minutes until soft. Add red chili powder and coriander. Serve hot with lemon wedges and tomatoes.

*Mauth is a smaller variety of mung beans.

Serving suggestion
Serve with besan halwa, toast, and coffee or masala chai.

Preferred kitchenware
• *Medium nonstick frying pan with lid*
• *2 qt. mixing bowl with lid*

Upma
South Indian Salty Snack
Serves 4

Preparation time: 30 mins.
Cooking time: 15 mins.

Ingredients:

6 tablespoons oil
$1/_2$ teaspoon mustard seeds
$1/_2$ teaspoon urad dal
5-6 curry leaves (karhi patta)
1 small onion, finely chopped
1 small green chili, finely chopped
1 cup semolina
3 cups warm water
1 teaspoon salt
2 tablespoons lemon juice
$1/_2$ teaspoon red chili powder
1 tablespoon coriander, chopped

Method:

Heat oil in pan on medium-high heat. Add mustard seeds and urad dal. When seeds start to pop, add curry leaves, onions and green chili. Cook for 3 minutes until soft, but not browned. Add semolina and cook for 3 minutes, stirring constantly.

Add water and keep stirring to prevent any lumps from forming. Add salt, lemon juice and red chili powder and stir again. Cover and leave on low heat for 5 minutes. Remove from heat and leave covered for another 10 minutes. Garnish with chopped coriander.

Serving suggestion
Serve with toast, fresh fruit, mathri, pickle, jalebi and masala chai.

Preferred kitchenware
• *Large nonstick frying pan with handle and lid*

Uttapam
South Indian Salty Pancake
Makes 8-10

Preparation time: 1 hr.
Cooking time: 5 mins. each

Ingredients:

2 cups semolina
1 teaspoon salt
1 cup yogurt
1¹/₂ cups water
1 medium onion, finely chopped
1 medium tomato, finely chopped
1 green chili, finely chopped
2 tablespoons coriander, chopped
For tempering:
1 tablespoon oil
1 teaspoon mustard seeds
8 curry leaves (karhi patta)

¹/₄ cup oil

Method:

Mix semolina, salt, yogurt and water. Let soak for one hour.
Add onion, tomato, green chili and coriander.
Tempering: Heat oil in small pan over medium heat. Add mustard seeds and curry leaves. Remove from heat when seeds start to pop. Add into semolina mixture.

Heat ¹/₂ tablespoon of oil in frying pan on medium heat. When hot, pour a large spoonful mixture into pan and spread with spoon into 8 inch round pancake. Cover for a few seconds. Spread about a teaspoon of oil on the surface and flip. Cook until golden brown on both sides.

Serving suggestion
Tastes great with coconut chutney and sambhar.

Preferred kitchenware
- *Large nonstick frying pan with handle and lid*
- *Small nonstick frying pan for tempering*
- *2 qt. mixing bowl with lid*

Tofu Bhurji
Spicy Scrambled Tofu
Serves 4

Preparation time: 30 mins.
Cooking time: 15 mins.

Ingredients:
16 ounces extra firm tofu
$2^1/_2$ tablespoons oil
1 small onion, chopped
1 small green chili, chopped
2 medium tomatoes, chopped
$^1/_2$ teaspoon salt
$^1/_4$ teaspoon red chili powder
$^1/_2$ teaspoon garam masala
2 tablespoons coriander, chopped

Method:
Drain tofu well. Pat dry with paper towel or cheesecloth to squeeze out any remaining water and crumble into small pieces.

Heat oil in frying pan on medium heat. Add onion and cook until transparent. Add green chili and tomatoes and cook for 2 minutes. Add tofu, salt, red chili powder, garam masala and coriander. Stir until well mixed. Cook for 2 minutes. Serve hot.

Serving suggestion
Serve with toast, coffee or masala chai.

Preferred kitchenware
• *Large nonstick frying pan*

Snacks and Chat

Alu Tikiya
Delicately Spiced Potato Patty
Makes 8

Preparation time: 1 hr.
Cooking time: 10 mins. per batch of four

Ingredients:
Tikiya (Patty):
2 slices of bread
4 medium sized boiled potatoes, peeled and mashed
$^3/_4$ teaspoon salt
$^1/_2$ teaspoon red chili powder
$^1/_2$ teaspoon garam masala
1 teaspoon pomegranate seeds, coarsely ground (optional)
$^1/_3$ cup oil
For garnish:
$^1/_2$ cup plain yogurt (mixed well)
Tamarind and/or mint coriander chutney
See recipe on page 140
$^1/_2$ teaspoon red chili powder
$^1/_2$ teaspoon cumin, roasted and ground
See recipe on page 173
2 tablespoons coriander, chopped

Method:
Remove crust from bread slices, dip bread in water and remove quickly. Mix with rest of the ingredients except oil in mixing bowl. Divide into 8 equal portions. Form into balls and flatten between palms to about $^1/_2$ inch thickness.
Heat half the oil on medium heat, for first batch of 4 patties. Shallow fry patties on both sides until deep golden brown. Repeat for second batch.
🍎*TLC Tip: While hot, add the garnishing ingredients proportionately and serve hot.*

Serving suggestion
Serve alone or with other chats.

Preferred kitchenware
• *1 qt. mixing bowl*
• *Tawa or nonstick frying pan*

Bhel Poori

Popular Snack from Mumbai

Serves 4

Preparation time: 20 mins.

Ingredients:

2 cups puffed rice (murmure)

$^1/_4$ cup fine sev*

$^1/_2$ cup Papri, coarsely crushed

See recipe on page 36

1 small onion, finely chopped

1 medium potato, boiled and cut into $^1/_2$ inch squares

$^1/_4$ teaspoon red chili powder

4 tablespoons tamarind chutney

See recipe on page 140

4 tablespoons mint coriander chutney

See recipe on page 140

1 tablespoon coriander, chopped

Method:

Place puffed rice in oven (200 degrees F) for 15 minutes to make it crisp. Toss with all dry ingredients.
Mix with remaining ingredients just before serving.

* Sev is a savory snack available at Indian grocery stores

Serving suggestion
Good for an 'any time snack'. Can also be served as an appetizer.

Preferred kitchenware
• *2 qt. mixing bowl*

Dahi Baday

Fried Dal Balls in Yogurt
Makes about 45 balls

Preparation time: 9 hrs.
Cooking time: 1 hr 30 mins.

Ingredients:

For Balls (Baday):
1 cup urad dal
$^3/_4$ cup water
$^1/_2$ teaspoon salt
Pinch of baking soda
2 cups oil

For Yogurt Mix:
1 $^1/_2$ cups plain yogurt
$^1/_2$ cup milk
$^1/_4$ cup water
$^1/_2$ teaspoon salt
$^1/_8$ teaspoon black salt (optional)
1 teaspoon sugar

For garnishing:
$^1/_4$ teaspoon cumin, roasted and ground
See recipe on page 173
$^1/_4$ teaspoon red chili powder
Tamarind chutney
See recipe on page 140

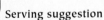

Serving suggestion
Serve with tamarind chutney as a snack or as a side dish with a meal.

Preferred kitchenware
- *Kadhai (or deep nonstick frying pan)*
- *Jharar (slotted spoon)*
- *Blender*
- *Medium mixing bowl*

Method:

Rinse and soak dal for 8 hours. Rinse again 3 to 4 times. Blend with $^3/_4$ cup of water into a fine paste. Add salt and baking soda.

Heat oil in kadhai or deep frying pan on medium-high heat. When oil is hot, drop about 10-12 cherry sized balls of dal paste into kadhai.

☙ *TLC Tip: Be sure to drop balls very close to the surface of oil, as oil can splatter and burn your fingertips.*

Continue turning balls until golden brown. Remove from kadhai and place on paper towel. Continue this procedure until all of dal mixture has been used.

Soak balls in hot water for 1 hour. Lightly whisk yogurt, milk and water in mixing bowl. Mix well to eliminate lumps. Add salt, black salt and sugar and set aside.

Gently squeeze out excess water from soaked balls and place in rectangular casserole dish. Pour yogurt mixture on top of balls and garnish with roasted ground cumin, red chili powder and tamarind chutney.

☙ *TLC Tip: When preparing baday in advance: After frying, let cool completely and store in freezer bags for up to two months.*

❗Caution: Use extreme care when deep frying. Due to a combination of factors, the object being fried may burst causing the hot oil to spatter. Some of the causes can be adding too much water, the oil being too hot, or the ingredients being old stock due to poor turnover in the store. It is always advisable to stand a fair distance away from the stove until you have made sure this is not happening. Also, you can hold a spatter screen as a safe guard.

❗Caution: Never leave the oil unattended over a stove. If overheated, the oil can catch fire, causing serious injury.

For help: www.momsindiancooking.com

Dhokla
Gujarati Snack
Serves 4

Preparation time: 45 mins.
Cooking time: 30 mins.

Ingredients:

Dhokla:
1 cup semolina
1 teaspoon salt
$1/_4$ teaspoon turmeric powder
1 teaspoon green chili, chopped
1 teaspoon ginger, grated
$1/_2$ cup yogurt
$1 \, 1/_2$ teaspoons oil
1 cup water
 For steaming:
3 cups water
For greasing:
1 teaspoon oil
1 teaspoon Eno fruit salt*
For tempering:
3 tablespoons oil
$1/_2$ teaspoon mustard seeds
4 medium green chilies, slit into fourths
5-6 curry leaves (karhi patta)
$1/_2$ teaspoon red chili powder
1 tablespoon coriander, chopped

*Available in Indian grocery stores

Serving suggestion
Serve as an appetizer for parties or as a snack.
Serve with mint-coriander chutney.

Preferred kitchenware
- *Round cake rack or steamer*
- *2 qt. mixing bowl*
- *8 qt. saucepan*
- *Small frying pan for tempering*
- *Round non stick cake pan*
- *Butter knife*

Method:
Mix all dhokla ingredients except Eno salt in bowl. Cover and let stand for 30 minutes.
Put cake rack or steamer at the bottom of saucepan. Add 3 cups water. Evenly grease cake pan with oil. Stir Eno salt into Dhokla mixture and pour into cake pan. Place cake pan over cake rack. Put saucepan on medium-high heat and let water come to a boil. Cover and steam for 10 minutes. *TLC Tip: To check if dhokla is done, prick with tooth pick. It should come out clean.*
Remove from heat. Let cool for 15 minutes. To remove dhokla from pan, go around edges with knife and turn the pan upside down over a plate. Cut into $1^1/_2$ inch square pieces.
Tempering: Heat oil in small frying pan on medium heat. Add mustard seeds. When they start to pop add other ingredients and remove from burner. Spread over dhoklas with a spoon. Garnish with chopped coriander.
TLC Tip: Red chili powder burns fast, therefore remember to turn stove off and remove from burner immediately after adding to oil.
TLC Tip: Dhoklas freeze well. Extra dhokla can be frozen in air tight containers for up to a month.

Gol Gappe

Also known as Pani Poori

Makes 70

Preparation time: 45 mins.
Cooking time: 1 hr.

Ingredients:

$^{1}/_{2}$ cup all-purpose flour
1 cup semolina
$^{1}/_{2}$ cup water
$1^{1}/_{2}$ cups oil

Method:

Mix flour and semolina and knead with water, added a little at a time, to make a hard dough. Set aside for $^{1}/_{2}$ hour. Knead again and divide into 70 pieces. Make small balls and roll to about $1^{1}/_{2}$ inch in diameter.

Heat oil in kadhai on medium-low temperature. Fry the round pieces of dough until golden brown. While frying, keep pressing pieces gently with slotted spoon so they puff up. Remove from oil and let cool on a paper towel.

! Caution: Never leave the oil unattended over a stove. If overheated, the oil can catch fire, causing serious injury.

Serving suggestion
To eat, make a small hole in the ball, fill with a few pieces of boiled and mashed potatoes, boiled chickpeas and jal jeera. Eat whole.

Preferred kitchenware
- *2 qt. mixing bowl*
- *Medium kadhai (or deep frying pan)*
- *Jharar (Slotted spoon)*
- *Rolling pin*

Jal Jeera

Jal Jeera translates to 'cumin water'. It can be a stand alone drink or an accompaniment to Gol Gappe

Serves 4

Preparation time: 30 mins.

Ingredients:

$^1/_2$ cup mint, chopped
$^1/_2$ cup coriander, chopped
1 teaspoon salt
$^1/_4$ teaspoon black salt
1 teaspoon cumin seeds, roasted and ground
See recipe on page 173
$^1/_4$ teaspoon red chili powder
Pinch of asafetida
2 teaspoons Pani Poori masala*
2 tablespoons sugar
1 medium green chili
Small piece of ginger, peeled
$^1/_2$ cup green mango, peeled and cut into very small cubes
1 tablespoon tamarind paste
3 cups water
$^1/_2$ fresh lemon, squeezed

Method:

Blend all ingredients except lemon into a fine paste with 1 cup of water. Add rest of the water and strain into a serving pitcher. Finally, add lemon juice and stir.

☙ *TLC Tip: When serving Jal Jeera as a party drink, garnish with fresh mint leaves.*

*Available in Indian grocery stores

Serving suggestion
This spicy beverage is usually served with Gol Gappe. Jal Jeera can also be served in small quantities as a party drink.

Preferred kitchenware
• *Blender*
• *Serving pitcher*
• *Strainer*

Mathari

North Indian Snack

Makes about 32

Preparation time: 45 mins.
Cooking time: 1hr.

Ingredients:

2 cups all purpose flour
1 cup semolina
1 teaspoon salt
$^1/_2$ cup oil (for dough)
4 ounces (exact) warm water
2-3 cups oil (for frying)

Serving Suggestion
Serve with tea or coffee and lemon pickle.

Preferred kitchenware
- *2 qt. mixing bowl*
- *Flour board*
- *Rolling pin*
- *Kadhai (or deep nonstick frying pan)*
- *Jharar (slotted spoon)*
- *Kitchen knife*

Method:

Mix flour, semolina, salt and $^1/_2$ cup of oil in bowl. Add a little water at a time, and knead until dough no longer sticks to bowl.

TLC Tip: It may help to put some oil on your hands to prevent the dough from sticking to your fingers.

Cover and leave for about 30 minutes.

Knead again and divide dough into 32 equal parts. Take each part and form into a ball. Press between your palms to flatten into about 1 inch diameter. Using a rolling pin, roll with moderate and uniform pressure to about $2^1/_2$ inches diameter. Make several $^1/_2$ inch long cuts with knife away from edges. This will prevent matharis from puffing up when frying. Have all matharis rolled out before heating oil.

Heat oil in kadhai over medium-low heat.

TLC Tip: To test the temperature, put a small drop of dough into oil. If it rises to top rapidly, oil is ready. If it stays at bottom or rises slowly, try again. Remove test pieces from oil before starting to fry.

Add about 6 matharis at a time.

TLC Tip: Slide in from the side, do not drop in the middle. Splattered oil can cause serious burns!

After 2-3 minutes, gently turn matharis. Keep repeating until they are light golden brown. Remove from kadhai. Cool and store in airtight container.

TLC Tip: For healthier version, use whole wheat flour instead of all purpose flour.

! Caution: Never leave the oil unattended over a stove. If overheated, the oil can catch fire, causing serious injury.

For help: www.momsindiancooking.com

Mung Dal Cheele*
Shallow Fried Mung Pan Cakes
Serves 4

Preparation time: 4 hrs. 30 mins.
Cooking time: 3 mins. per cheela**

Ingredients:

$1^1/_2$ cups mung dal
$1^1/_4$ cups water
1 teaspoon salt
$^1/_2$ teaspoon red chili powder
2 tablespoons coriander, chopped
$^1/_4$ cup oil

Method:

Rinse and soak dal for 4 hours. Drain and grind in blender with $1^1/_4$ cups of water. Combine ground dal, salt, red chili powder, and coriander in mixing bowl.

Heat 1 tablespoon of oil in frying pan on medium-high heat. Put approximately $^1/_4$ cup of dal mixture into frying pan and spread it with a circular motion using the back of a rounded spoon to create a pancake 6 inch in diameter. Sprinkle 1 teaspoon of oil on the top surface. Lift the edge of cheela gently, and if it does not stick, it is ready to be turned over. Cook until golden brown on both sides.

* *Pronounced chee-lay (plural)*
***Pronounced chee-laa (singular)*

Serving Suggestion
Serve hot with mint and coriander chutney, yogurt, and lemon pickle.

Preferred kitchenware
- *Blender*
- *Medium sized mixing bowl*
- *Rounded cooking spoon*
- *Medium nonstick frying pan*

For help: www.momsindiancooking.com

Pao Bhaji

Pao is a kind of bun and Bhaji means cooked vegetables. The popularity of this roadside dish from Mumbai has increased many folds over the years because of its spicy/ tangy flavor.

Serves 4

Preparation time: 1 hr.
Cooking time: 25 mins.

Ingredients:

Bhaji:
$1/2$ cup fresh green beans
1 large piece of cauliflower
2 carrots
$1/2$ bell pepper
1 medium onion
2 large tomatoes
Lemon-onion mixture:
$1/4$ teaspoon salt
1 small onion, finely chopped
4 tablespoons lemon juice

4 tablespoons oil
$3/4$ teaspoon salt
3 tablespoons Pao Bhaji masala*
3 large potatoes, boiled and crumbled
$1/2$ cup water
1 tablespoon butter
2 tablespoons coriander, chopped
2 $1/2$ tablespoons lemon juice

8 Hamburger buns
*Available in Indian grocery stores

Method:

Wash and cut vegetables into small pieces (about $1/4$ inch thick). Keep onions and tomatoes aside. Place vegetables (other than onions and tomatoes) in microwaveable bowl, cover and steam in microwave for about 7 minutes.

Lemon onion mixture: In a separate bowl, put onions. Add salt and lemon juice. Mix and set aside.

Heat oil in frying pan on medium-high heat. Add onions and stir for 2 minutes. Add tomatoes. Cook for 2 to 3 minutes. Add steamed vegetables, salt and Pao Bhaji masala. Cook for 3 to 4 minutes. Add potatoes and water. Stir. Cover and reduce heat to low. Add butter, cook for 10 minutes, stirring occasionally. Add coriander and lemon juice.
Slice buns in half and toast lightly in toaster oven or lightly brown in frying pan with light coating of oil/butter.

Serving suggestion
Heap bhaji on bun and add lemon onion mixture to taste.

Preferred kitchenware
• *Large nonstick frying pan with lid*
• *Medium microwave safe bowl with lid*
• *Medium mixing bowl*

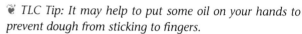

Papri Chat
Flour Chips with Yogurt and Chutney

Serves 4

Preparation time: 1 hr 30 mins.
Cooking time: 1 hr.

Ingredients:

Papri (Traditional):
$^1/_2$ cup all purpose flour
1 cup semolina
$^1/_2$ cup warm water
$1^1/_2$ cups oil
Papri (Short Cut):
4 big (burrito size) tortillas cut
into $^3/_4$ inch square pieces

Chat:
1 cup yogurt, plain
$^1/_4$ cup water
$^1/_4$ teaspoon salt
2 small potatoes, boiled and cut
into $^1/_2$ inch squares
4 tablespoons coriander chutney
See recipe page 140
$^1/_4$ cup tamarind chutney
See recipe page 140
$^1/_2$ teaspoon cumin, roasted and ground
See recipe on page 173
$^1/_4$ teaspoon red chili powder
4 tablespoons sev*
1 tablespoon coriander, chopped

Method:

Mix and knead flour and semolina to make a
firm dough with $^1/_2$ cup warm water.

* Sev is a savory snack available at Indian grocery stores

❦ *TLC Tip: It may help to put some oil on your hands to
prevent dough from sticking to fingers.*
Set aside for 30 minutes. Divide into 70 parts. Make
balls and roll to about $1^1/_2$ inch diameter pieces. With
a knife, make a few slits in middle of each so they do
not puff up when frying.
Heat oil in kadhai on medium-low heat.
❦*TLC Tip: To test the temperature, put a small drop of dough
or small piece of tortilla into oil. If it rises rapidly, oil is ready.
If it stays at bottom or rises slowly, try again.*

Remove the test pieces from the oil before starting to
fry. Fry tortillas or the small rounds pieces from
traditional recipe, until golden brown. Let cool.
❦ *TLC Tip: Slide in from the side. Do not drop in the middle.
Splashed oil can cause serious burns.*

Lightly whisk yogurt, water and salt in mixing bowl.
Make sure there are no lumps. In a long serving plate,
arrange tortilla pieces or Papris. Add yogurt mixture,
potatoes, both chutneys and sprinkle with roasted,
ground cumin, chili powder, sev and coriander.

Serving suggestion
*Serve immediately to prevent dish from
becoming soggy.*

Preferred kitchenware
• *2 qt. mixing bowl*
• *Kadhai (or deep nonstick frying pan)*
• *Rolling pin*

Saboodana Khichadi

Tapioca Snack
Serves 4

Preparation time: 3 hrs.
Cooking time: 5-10 mins.

Ingredients:

1$^1/_2$ cups tapioca
$^3/_4$ cup water
1 teaspoon salt
$^1/_8$ teaspoon turmeric powder
$^1/_2$ teaspoon red chili powder
$^1/_2$ cup unsalted peanuts, roasted and crushed
1 small green chili, chopped
2$^1/_2$ tablespoons oil
1 tablespoon lemon juice
$^1/_2$ teaspoon sugar
2 tablespoons coriander, chopped

Method:

Rinse tapioca 2 to 3 times and let it soak in $^3/_4$ cup of water for 3 hours, stirring 2 to 3 times in between. Add salt, turmeric powder, red chili powder, peanuts and green chili to tapioca and mix.
Heat oil on medium-heat. Add tapioca mixture. Cook for 6 to 7 minutes, stirring continuously. Add lemon juice and sugar. Stir for another minute. Check to make sure tapioca is soft and remove from heat. Garnish with chopped coriander.
Note: If observing a religious fast, replace red chili powder with crushed black pepper.

Serving suggestion
An any time snack, great with masala chai.

Preferred kitchenware
• *Nonstick frying pan*
• *Medium mixing bowl*

Vegetable Pakoda
Vegetable Fritters
Serves 4

Preparation time: 45 mins.
Cooking time: 30 mins.

Ingredients:
1 cup gram flour (besan)
$^2/_3$ cup water
$^1/_2$ teaspoon salt
$^1/_4$ teaspoon turmeric powder
$^1/_2$ teaspoon red chili powder
2 cups oil
Pinch of baking soda
Thinly sliced, or small pieces of paneer and vegetables such as potatoes, green pepper, onion, cauliflower, spinach and egg plant

Method:
Mix gram flour with water, salt, turmeric powder and red chili powder. Stir well to remove all lumps. Set aside and let stand for 10 minutes.
Heat oil in kadhai on medium-high heat. Add baking soda to mixture of gram flour.

🐞 *TLC Tip: To test the temperature put a small drop of pakoda mix into oil. If it rises rapidly, oil is ready. If it stays at bottom or rises slowly, try again.*

Serving suggestion
Delicious as a hot snack with tea. In India, they are particularly enjoyable during monsoon.

Preferred kitchenware
- *2 qt. mixing bowl*
- *Kadhai (or deep nonstick frying pan)*
- *Jharar (slotted spoon)*

Remove test pieces from oil. Take each piece of vegetable, dip in batter and add to oil continuously and swiftly until about 10-12 pakodas are in oil.

🐞 *TLC Tip: Do not drop from a height of more than 1 inch. Otherwise hot oil may splatter and cause burns.*

Turn pakodas over few times until golden brown. Take the pakodas out with slotted spoon and drain the oil thoroughly by lightly tapping the spoon on the inside edge of kadhai. Put pakodas on a paper towel to absorb excess oil. Repeat with the rest of the mixture.

🐞 *TLC Tip: If at anytime the oil starts to smoke or the pakodas begin to turn black, reduce heat and wait until temperature is right and resume.*

⚠ **Caution: Use extreme care when deep frying. Due to a combination of factors, the object being fried may burst causing the hot oil to spatter. Some of the causes can be adding too much water, the oil being too hot, or the ingredients being old stock due to poor turnover in the store. It is always advisable to stand a fair distance away from the stove until you have made sure this is not happening. Also, you can hold a spatter screen as a safe guard.**

For help: www.momsindiancooking.com

Vegetable &
other Side Dishes

Amras

Mango Side Dish

Serves 4

Preparation time: 10 mins.

Ingredients:

2 tablespoons sugar
30 oz. can mango pulp
or equal amount of fresh mango pulp
1 cup milk
1 teaspoon cardamom, ground

Method:

Mix sugar, mango pulp and milk. If using fresh mangos, peel, discard seed and blend into a puree. Add cardamom. Serve chilled in glass bowls.

Serving suggestion
Sweet mango side dish to accompany any meal, especially a meal with pooris.

Preferred kitchenware
- *1 qt. mixing bowl*
- *Blender- if using fresh mangos*

Anannas Subzi

Pineapple in Light Spicy Sauce
Serves 4

Preparation time: 10 mins.
Cooking time: 15 mins.

Ingredients:

1 (20 ounce) can unsweetened pineapple chunks
1 tablespoon oil
$1/4$ teaspoon cumin seeds
$1/4$ teaspoon turmeric powder
$1/2$ teaspoon salt
$1/4$ teaspoon red chili powder
$1/2$ teaspoon dry mango powder (amchur)
$1/4$ teaspoon garam masala
2 tablespoons coriander, chopped

Method:

Keep open can of pineapple ready.
Heat oil in saucepan over medium-high heat. Add cumin seeds. When seeds start to pop add turmeric powder and pineapple (with juice). Stir and add rest of ingredients. When mixture comes to a boil, reduce heat to low and cover. Let cook for 10 minutes on low heat.
Garnish with chopped coriander.

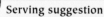

Serving suggestion
Serve with Matar or Gobhi and plain paranthas.

Preferred kitchenware
• *$1^1/_2$ qt. saucepan with lid*

Baigan Bhartha
Spicy Roasted Eggplant
Serves 4

Preparation time: 30 mins.
Cooking time: 15 mins.

Ingredients:

1 eggplant (large)*
4 tablespoons oil
$^1/_2$ teaspoon cumin seeds
1 medium onion, chopped**
1 tablespoon green chili, chopped
1 tablespoon ginger, finely chopped
2 medium fresh tomatoes**
or 5 tablespoons canned crushed tomatoes**
1 teaspoon salt
$^1/_2$ teaspoon turmeric powder**
$^1/_2$ teaspoon red chili powder**
2 teaspoons coriander powder**
$^1/_2$ teaspoon garam masala **
$^1/_8$ cup water
2 tablespoons coriander, chopped

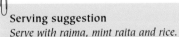

Serving suggestion
Serve with rajma, mint raita and rice.

Preferred kitchenware
• *Medium nonstick frying pan*
• *Microwave safe bowl*

Method:

Wash eggplant and cut off both ends. Prick in a few places with a sharp knife. Wrap in plastic bag. Microwave in bowl at full heat for 12 minutes. Make sure it is soft to the core when taken out. Remove from bag and place in bowl. Slit lengthwise from the middle, take all pulp*** out and discard skin. Mash the pulp with a spoon.

Heat oil in pan over medium-high heat. Add cumin seeds. When seeds start to pop, add onions, green chili, ginger, and cook for 5 minutes. Add tomatoes and other spices. Cook for another 5 minutes. Add eggplant pulp and water and reduce heat to low. Stir, cover and let cook for another 5 minutes. Garnish with chopped coriander.

* ❧ *TLC Tip: The eggplant should feel light. This indicates that it does not have too many seeds.*

** *For traditional less spicy version, do not use these ingredients.*

*** ❧ *TLC Tip: The pulp can be frozen in air tight containers for future use.*

Besan Ki Mirch - Bharvan
Peppers Stuffed with Gram Flour
Serves 4

Preparation time: 15 mins.
Cooking time: 30 mins.

Ingredients:

6 tablespoons oil (for roasting gram flour)
$1^1/_2$ cups gram flour (besan)
1 teaspoon salt
$^1/_2$ teaspoon turmeric powder (for filling)
$^3/_4$ teaspoon red chili powder
3 teaspoons coriander powder
2 teaspoons dry mango powder (amchur)
4 teaspoons fennel seeds, coarsely ground
8 - five to six inch long Italian green peppers (mild)
6 tablespoons water
2 tablespoons oil (for sautéing)
$^1/_4$ teaspoon turmeric powder (for sautéing)

Serving suggestion
Tastes great with plain paranthas!

Preferred kitchenware
• *Nonstick frying pan*

Method:

Heat 6 tablespoons of oil in pan on medium-high heat. Add gram flour. Cook, stirring constantly, until it turns golden brown. Turn heat off and add all ingredients except remaining oil, water and $^1/_4$ teaspoon turmeric powder. Mix well and let cool for 15 minutes.

Wash peppers and slit them down the middle on one side only. When gram flour is cool, add water and mix. Fill peppers with gram flour mixture. Heat 2 tablespoons of oil in frying pan on medium heat. Add turmeric powder and peppers and keep turning until golden brown on all sides (about 5 minutes).

Bhindi Masala
Spicy Okra
Serves 4

Preparation time: 30 mins.
Cooking time: 10 mins.

Ingredients:

2 pounds fresh okra
3 tablespoons oil
$^1/_4$ teaspoon cumin seeds
Pinch of asafetida
$^1/_4$ teaspoon turmeric powder
1 teaspoon salt
$^3/_4$ teaspoon red chili powder
2 teaspoons coriander powder
1 teaspoon dry mango powder (amchur)
2 tablespoons coriander, chopped
Optional for party version:
1 large onion, sliced
1 large tomato, sliced

Method:

Wash okra and thoroughly dry with paper towel or clean dish towel.
🌶 *TLC Tip: It will be a gooey mess if okras are not dry before cutting!*.
Cut and discard about $^1/_4$ inch from both ends. Slice lengthwise into halves, or cut $^1/_2$ inch round slices.

Heat oil in pan over medium heat. Add cumin seeds, asafetida, and turmeric powder. When cumin seeds start to pop, add okra and salt. Stir and cover. Reduce heat to medium-low, cooking until okra gets soft, stirring occasionally. Add rest of spices. Reduce heat to low and let cook for 5 minutes. Garnish with chopped coriander.

Party version: Follow the above, except, before adding okra, sauté onions until golden brown. Add tomatoes and cook for 2-3 minutes. You may increase the amount of oil to give that 'restaurant' look.
Stuffed variety: Instead of cutting okra in halves, slit them lengthwise on one side. Stuff with all the spices (other than cumin seeds and asafetida) and follow the above method.

Serving suggestion
Serve okra with plain paranthas and matar paneer, or dal makhani.

Preferred kitchenware
• *Nonstick frying pan with lid*

Chatpate Alu
Spicy Potato from Uttar Pradesh
Serves 4

Preparation time: 15 mins.
Cooking time: 25 mins.

Ingredients:

4 medium potatoes (preferably oblong)
3 tablespoons mustard oil (preferred)
or other cooking oil
$^1/_2$ teaspoon cumin seeds
2 whole red dried chilies
$^1/_4$ teaspoon turmeric powder
2 heaping teaspoons coriander powder
$^1/_4$ teaspoon red chili powder
2 cups water
1 teaspoon salt
1 heaping teaspoon dry mango powder (amchur)
$^1/_4$ teaspoon garam masala
For tempering:
1 tablespoon oil
1/4 teaspoon paprika

1 tablespoon coriander, chopped

Method:

Thoroughly scrub and wash potatoes. Do not peel. Cut into vertical slices about twice the thickness of average french fries.

Heat mustard oil in saucepan on medium-high heat. Add cumin seeds and whole red chilies. When cumin seeds start to pop, add turmeric powder and coriander powder. Roast ingredients for 1 to 2 minutes. Add red chili powder, potatoes, water and salt. Stir and turn heat to high until mixture starts to boil. Reduce heat to medium-low and cover. Stir occasionally until potatoes become tender (takes about 15-17 minutes).

Add dry mango powder and garam masala and reduce heat to low.

In small frying pan add the other tablespoon of oil and paprika and fry on medium heat stirring constantly until paprika turns dark red. Add this oil mixture to potatoes.

🍎 *TLC Tip: To scoop up all of this mixture pour some of the liquid from the potatoes into frying pan, stir and add back to potatoes.*

Turn heat off and garnish with chopped coriander.

Serving suggestion
Serve with kachori and/or poori with fried ginger on the side.

Preferred kitchenware
• *4 qt. saucepan with lid*
• *Very small frying pan*

Chhole
Spicy Chickpeas from the Punjab
Serves 4

Preparation time: 9 hrs.
Cooking time: 25 mins. (pressure cooker)
            60 mins. (saucepan)

Ingredients:
1 cup dry chickpeas
1 teaspoon salt
3 cups water
1 teaspoon cumin powder, roasted
See recipe on page 173
1 teaspoon red chili powder
4 teaspoons coriander powder
2 teaspoons dry mango powder (amchur)
1 teaspoon garam masala
3 tablespoons pomegranate seed powder, roasted
See recipe on page 173
2 tablespoons ginger, peeled and sliced thinly along the length (about $1/_8$ inch by $1/_8$ inch)
2 small green chilies, thinly slit along the length
4 tablespoons oil
For garnish:
1 medium tomato, cut into wedges
1 medium onion, cut into wedges
2 tablespoons coriander, chopped

Method:
Soak chickpeas for 8 hours. Rinse. Put pressure cooker on medium high heat add chickpeas, salt and three cups of water. Close lid and put weight on. After pressure builds up, turn heat on low and cook for a total of about 12 minutes (or till chickpeas get soft).
❦ *TLC Tip: Put pressure cooker under cold running water before opening to reduce pressure.*
❦ *TLC Tip: If you do not have a pressure cooker, add 4 cups of water, chickpeas and salt to sauce pan and put on high*

heat until the mixture comes to a boil. Turn heat to low and continue boiling for about 45-50 minutes or until chickpeas turn tender. Keep half covered with lid during the process.

Drain about half of the water out and put aside. Place pressure cooker back on medium heat and add cumin, red chilli, coriander, mango, garam masala, pomegranate seed power, ginger and green chilies on top of chickpea mixture. DO NOT STIR.

Heat oil in a small frying pan until very hot. Pour over ingredients in pressure cooker and stir. Turn heat on low and cook for another 5 minutes. If more sauce is preferred, add some of the water drained initially and put aside.

Garnish with tomato, onion wedges and chopped coriander.

❦ *TLC Tip: Canned chickpeas can also be used in this recipe.*
❦ *TLC Tip: Extra chickpeas can be frozen in air tight containers for future use.*

Serving suggestion
Serve with bhatura and salad. Plain or salty lassi goes well with it.

Preferred kitchenware
- *4 qt. pressure cooker or 4 qt. sauce pan with lid*
- *Small frying pan*

Dahi ke Alu

Potato Subzi with Yogurt Sauce

Serves 4

Preparation time: 10 mins.
Cooking time: 25 mins.

Ingredients:

4 medium potatoes
4 tablespoons plain yogurt
1 cup water
1 tablespoon oil
$^1/_4$ teaspoon cumin seeds
4 whole cloves
$^1/_4$ teaspoon turmeric powder
$^1/_4$ teaspoon red chili powder
1 teaspoon salt
$^1/_2$ teaspoon garam masala
1 tablespoon coriander, chopped

Method:

Boil potatoes until soft. Peel and crush into small pieces by hand. Whisk yogurt and water until no lumps remain.

Heat oil in pan over medium-high heat. Add cumin seeds and cloves. When seeds start to pop, add turmeric powder, red chili powder, yogurt mix and potatoes. Stir until mixture comes to a boil.

❦ *TLC Tip: Constant stirring is very important, otherwise yogurt will separate from mixture.*

Add salt and garam masala and reduce heat to low and cook for another 8 minutes. Garnish with chopped coriander.

Serving suggestion
Serve with plain paranthas and a green vegetable.

Preferred kitchenware
• *1$^1/_2$ qt. saucepan with lid*

Dum Alu

Fried Whole Potato in Tomato Sauce

Serves 4

Preparation time: 15 mins.
Cooking time: 30 mins.

Ingredients:

8 small potatoes
$1^1/_2$ cups oil
$^1/_2$ cup precooked masala
See recipe on page 172
$^3/_4$ cup water
$^1/_2$ teaspoon salt
$^1/_4$ teaspoon turmeric powder
$^1/_4$ teaspoon red chili powder
2 tablespoons plain yogurt (smoothed)
$^1/_2$ teaspoon garam masala
2 tablespoons coriander, chopped

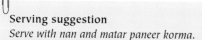

Serving suggestion
Serve with nan and matar paneer korma.

Preferred kitchenware
- *$1^1/_2$ qt. saucepan*
- *Kadhai or medium frying pan*

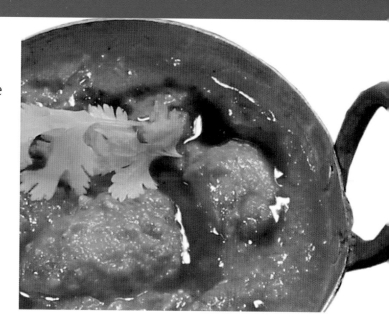

Method:

Boil potatoes on medium-high heat for about 10 minutes, making sure that they are only $^3/_4$ cooked. Put in cold water and peel. Prick with fork several times.

Heat oil in kadhai/frying pan and fry potatoes until golden brown. Turn off heat. Remove and put aside. Place sauce pan on medium-high heat. Add precooked masala, water, salt, turmeric powder, red chili powder and potatoes. When mixture comes to a boil, turn heat to low and add yogurt and garam masala. Stir. Cook another 5 minutes.

Before serving, garnish with coriander.

❦ *TLC Tip: Use a 14 ounce can of whole new potatoes as a substitute for fresh potatoes. If too big, cut into halves. Canned potatoes do not have to be boiled.*

Fruit Chat
Spicy Fruit Salad
Serves 4

Preparation time: 15 mins

Ingredients:
1 banana, thinly sliced
1 pear, cut into small cubes
1 cucumber, peeled and cut into small cubes
1 medium tomato, cut into small cubes
1 guava, cut into small cubes (if available)
1 mango, peeled and cut in to small cubes (if available)
5–6 Ripe strawberries, thinly sliced
1 tablespoon sugar
1 teaspoon cumin, roasted and ground
See recipe on page 173
$1/_2$ teaspoon salt
$1/_2$ teaspoon black pepper, ground
OR
$1/_4$ teaspoon red chili powder
3 tablespoons lemon juice

Method:
Gently mix all ingredients in bowl.

Serving suggestions
Serve with dinner as a side dish or as a snack.

Preferred kitchenware
• *1 medium mixing bowl*

Gobhi Alu
Cauliflower and Potatoes
Serves 4

Preparation time: 20 mins.
Cooking time: 20 mins.

Ingredients:
5 tablespoons oil
$^1/_4$ teaspoon cumin seeds
Pinch of asafetida
$^1/_4$ teaspoon turmeric powder
1 tablespoon ginger, finely chopped
(optional)
1 cauliflower, cut into two inch pieces
2 medium potatoes, peeled and cut
into one inch pieces
1 teaspoon salt
$^1/_2$ teaspoon red chili powder
2 teaspoons coriander powder
1 teaspoon dry mango powder (amchur)
$^1/_2$ teaspoon garam masala
2 tablespoons coriander, chopped

Method:
Heat oil in pan over medium heat, add cumin seeds,
asafetida, turmeric powder and ginger. When cumin
seeds start to pop, add cauliflower, potatoes and salt.

Stir and cover. Cook until cauliflower and potatoes
get soft, stirring occasionally. Add rest of the spices,
reduce heat to low and let cook for another 5 minutes.
Garnish with chopped coriander.

*Note: You can use this recipe for items such as spinach alu,
methi alu, green beans and alu, cabbage and alu, matar
alu, etc.*
*For **spinach alu**, use 10 ounces frozen spinach and 4
medium potatoes.*
*For **methi alu**, use 2 pounds of methi leaves washed and
chopped and 4 medium potatoes.*
*For **cabbage and alu**, use 1 small cabbage, washed and
chopped and 2 medium potatoes.*
*For **green beans and alu**, use 1 pound green beans, washed
and chopped and 4 medium potatoes.*
*For **matar and alu**, use $1^1/_2$ cups peas, thawed and 4
medium potatoes.*

Serving suggestion
*Serve with dal and roti or raita and
parantha.*

Preferred kitchenware
• *Nonstick frying pan with lid*

Jhunko

Konkani Style Bell Pepper with Gram
Flour

Serves 4

Preparation time: 20 mins.
Cooking time: 10 mins.

Ingredients:

2 tablespoons oil (for roasting)
$^1/_2$ cup gram flour (besan)
5 tablespoons oil (for cooking)
1 teaspoon mustard seeds
Pinch of asafetida
1 large onion, chopped
1 green bell pepper, chopped into 1 inch pieces
1 red bell pepper, chopped into 1 inch pieces
$^3/_4$ teaspoon salt
$^1/_2$ teaspoon turmeric powder
1 teaspoon sugar
$^1/_2$ teaspoon red chili powder

Method:

Heat oil for roasting in pan over medium heat. Add
gram flour. Roast gram flour until it turns golden brown
and remove from pan.
Place pan back on medium heat and add remaining
oil. Add mustard seeds and asafetida. When seeds start
to pop, add onions. Sauté until pink. Add bell peppers,
salt, turmeric powder and sugar. Cook uncovered on
medium-low heat until bell peppers are a little soft. Add
roasted gram flour mixture and red chili powder. Stir.
Cook for another 2 minutes.

Serving suggestion
Tastes great with plain paranthas.

Preferred kitchenware
• *Non-stick frying pan*

Kaddu

Spicy Pumpkin

Serves 4

Preparation time: 30 mins.
Cooking time: 25 mins.

Ingredients:

1 pound pumpkin or butternut squash
3 tablespoons oil
$^1/_2$ teaspoon cumin seeds
$^3/_4$ teaspoon mustard seeds
$1^1/_2$ teaspoon turmeric powder
$1^1/_4$ teaspoons salt
1 tablespoon green chilies, chopped
1 tablespoon ginger, chopped
$^3/_4$ cup water
$^1/_2$ teaspoon red chili powder
$2^1/_2$ tablespoons coriander powder
$2^1/_2$ tablespoons dry mango powder (amchur)
2 tablespoons sugar
2 tablespoons coriander, chopped

Method:

Remove skin and seeds from pumpkin or squash and cut into 1 inch by 1 inch by $^1/_2$ inch pieces.

Heat oil in pan over medium high heat. Add cumin seeds, mustard seeds and turmeric powder. When cumin seeds start to pop, add pumpkin or squash, salt, green chili, and ginger. Add water. Stir and reduce heat to medium low. Cover and cook for 15 to 20 minutes or until it gets soft, stirring occasionally. Add remaining ingredients except coriander. Stir. Turn heat off. Garnish with chopped coriander.

Serving suggestion
Serve with poori, plain parantha or kachori along with chatpate alu.

Preferred kitchenware
• *Large nonstick frying pan with lid.*

Karela - Bharvan
Stuffed Bitter Melon
Serves 4

Preparation time: 4 hrs.
Cooking time: 35 mins.

Ingredients:

8 medium size bitter melons
2 teaspoons salt (for marinating)
1 tablespoon oil (for roasting spices)
1 teaspoon red chili powder
4 tablespoons coriander powder
$1^1/_2$ teaspoons dry mango powder (amchur)
2 tablespoons fennel seeds, crushed
4 tablespoons oil (for cooking)
$^1/_2$ teaspoon turmeric powder
$^1/_2$ teaspoon salt
3 tablespoons water

Method:

Thoroughly wash and peel bitter melons. Cut about
1/4 inches from both ends and discard ends. Slit length
wise on one side only. Rub with salt inside and out.
Keep aside for 3 hours. Wash thoroughly and squeeze
out excess water. Heat 1 tablespoon oil in pan or kadhai
on medium heat. Add spices (other than salt and
turmeric powder) and roast for 2 to 3 minutes. Remove
from heat and let cool.

Stuff bitter melons with roasted spices and put aside.
Heat oil in pan/kadhai on medium heat, add turmeric
powder and bitter melons. Stir gently. Sprinkle $^1/_2$
teaspoon salt on top. Add 3 tablespoons water. Cover
and leave on low heat stirring gently occasionally. Cook
until golden brown and tender.

❦ *TLC Tip: Extra karelas can be frozen in air tight containers
for future use.*

Serving suggestion
*Serve with plain paranthas and/or
basmati rice and karhi.*

Preferred kitchenware
• *Medium nonstick frying pan with lid
or medium kadhai.*

Karela - Quick Version

Spicy Bitter Melon

Serves 4

Preparation time: 4 hrs.
Cooking time: 15 mins.

Ingredients:

8 medium bitter melons
2 teaspoons salt (for marinating)
2 cups oil (for frying)
2 tablespoons oil (to sauté onions)
1 large onion, thinly sliced
$^1/_2$ teaspoon salt
$^1/_2$ teaspoon turmeric powder
1 teaspoon red chili powder
4 tablespoons coriander powder
$1^1/_2$ teaspoons dry mango powder (amchur)
2 tablespoons fennel seeds, crushed

Method:

Thoroughly wash and peel bitter melons. Cut about $^1/_4$ inch from both ends and discard ends. Cut into thin (about $^1/_4$ inch thick) round slices. Rub with salt. Keep aside for 3 hours. Wash thoroughly and squeeze out excess water.

Heat oil in kadhai over medium heat and fry bitter melon slices until golden brown.

Heat 2 tablespoons of oil in frying pan over medium heat. Sauté onions until golden brown. Mix other spices and roast for 2 minutes. Add bitter melons, stir, cover and cook for 5 minutes on medium low heat.

Serving suggestion
Serve with plain paranthas and/or basmati rice and karhi.

Preferred kitchenware
• *Nonstick frying pan with lid.*
• *Medium kadhai*

Kathal Subzi

Spicy Jack Fruit
Serves 4

Preparation time: 15 mins.
Cooking time: 10 mins.

Ingredients:
1 (about 20 oz) canned jackfruit
3 tablespoons oil
$^1/_4$ teaspoon cumin seeds
Pinch of asafetida
$^1/_4$ teaspoon turmeric powder
$^1/_2$ teaspoon salt
$^1/_2$ teaspoon red chili powder
$1^1/_2$ teaspoons coriander powder
1 teaspoon dry mango powder (amchur)
2 tablespoons coriander, chopped

Method:
Drain liquid from can using a large strainer and rinse jackfruit with water. Leave in strainer to drain for 10 minutes.

Heat oil in pan over medium heat. Add cumin seeds, asafetida and turmeric powder. When cumin seeds, start to pop, add jackfruit, salt and other spices. Stir, cover and reduce heat to low. Cook for 5 to 7 minutes, stirring occasionally.

Garnish with chopped coriander before serving.

Serving Suggestions
Kathal comes closest to a non vegetarian dish in taste. Can be used as a side dish with any meal, preferably with paranthas.

Preferred kitchenware
- *Nonstick frying pan with lid*
- *Large strainer*

Malai Kofta
Cheese Balls in Cream Sauce
Serves 4

Preparation time: 3 hrs 30 mins.
Cooking time: 20 mins.

Ingredients:

Kofta (Cheese Balls):
8 ounces ricotta cheese
2 medium potatoes, boiled and finely mashed
$^1/_2$ teaspoon salt
$^1/_4$ teaspoon garam masala
1 tablespoon powdered milk
$1^1/_2$ tablespoons corn flour
1 tablespoon all-purpose flour (for mixing)
3 tablespoons all-purpose flour (for rolling)
2 cups oil (for frying)
For sauce:
1 cup precooked masala
See recipe on page 172
2 $^1/_4$ cups water
$^1/_2$ pint heavy cream
$^1/_2$ teaspoon salt
$^1/_4$ teaspoon red chili powder
$^1/_4$ teaspoon garam masala
1 teaspoon sugar
2 tablespoons coriander, chopped

Serving suggestion
Serve with tandoori roti along with other party dishes.

Preferred kitchenware
- *Kadhai or deep frying pan*
- *2qt. sauce pan*
- *1qt. mixing bowl*
- *Cheesecloth*
- *Large strainer*

Method:

Kofta: Strain out excess water from ricotta cheese by placing over cheesecloth inside large strainer (takes 2 to 3 hours).
Mix ricotta cheese and all other ingredients for kofta (except 3 tablespoons all-purpose flour) in bowl. Make about 10 oval shaped balls and roll in remaining flour.
Heat oil in kadhai over medium heat. When hot, fry 3 to 4 koftas at a time until golden brown. Put aside.

Sauce: Heat saucepan over medium-high heat. Add precooked masala and water to pan. When mixture comes to a boil, add cream, salt, chili powder, garam masala, sugar, and continue stirring. Reduce heat to low and cook for another 10 minutes. Add koftas, stir once, turn heat off and keep covered.
Before serving, garnish with chopped coriander.
🌿 *TLC Tip: The balls can be made ahead of time and frozen in air tight containers or freezer bags for later use.*

Caution: Never leave oil unattended over a stove. If overheated, the oil can catch fire, causing serious injury

Matar Paneer

Peas and Cheese with Tomato Sauce

Serves 4

Preparation time: 15 mins.
Cooking time: 20 mins.

Ingredients:

1 cup frozen peas, thawed
$^1/_2$ cup precooked masala
See recipe on page 172
1 $^1/_4$ cups water
$^1/_2$ teaspoon salt
1 cup fried paneer cubes
See recipe on page 171
$^1/_4$ teaspoon garam masala
$^1/_2$ teaspoon sugar
2 tablespoons coriander, chopped

Method:

Place pan on medium high, add peas, precooked masala, water and salt. When mixture comes to a boil, add paneer. Reduce heat to medium-low and cook for 10 minutes partially covered and stirring occasionally. Add garam masala and sugar. Stir, turn heat off and keep covered.
Before serving, garnish with coriander.

Serving suggestion
This delicious party dish goes well with boondi raita, gobhi alu and parantha or nan.

Preferred kitchenware
• $1^1/_2$ qt. saucepan

Matar Paneer Korma

Peas and Crumbled Cheese with Tomato Masala

Serves 4

Preparation time: 20 mins.
Cooking time: 20 mins.

Ingredients:

1 tablespoon oil
$1^1/_2$ cups paneer, crumbled
See recipe on page 171
1 cup peas, fresh or frozen (thawed)
$^3/_4$ cup precooked masala
See recipe on page 172
$^1/_4$ cup water
$^1/_2$ teaspoon salt
$^1/_2$ cup cashew nuts, fried golden brown
$^1/_2$ teaspoon garam masala
1 teaspoon sugar
2 tablespoons coriander, chopped

Method:

Heat oil in pan over medium heat. Add paneer and stir for 5 minutes. Add peas, precooked masala, water and salt. Stir and cover. Cook on low heat for 5 to 7 minutes, stirring occasionally. Add cashew nuts, garam masala and sugar. Cover and cook for another 5 minutes. Before serving, garnish with chopped coriander.

Serving suggestion
This delicious party dish goes well with boondi raita, dum alu and parantha or nan.

Preferred kitchenware
• *Medium frying pan with lid*

Mirch ke Tapore

Rajasthani Dish of Sautéd Green Chili, Traditionally Served in Rural Feasts

Preparation time: 15 mins.
Cooking time: 10 mins.

Ingredients:

3 tablespoons oil
$^3/_4$ teaspoon mustard seeds
$^1/_2$ teaspoon turmeric powder
1 lb hot green chili pepper (about 5-6 inches long), chopped into $^1/_2$ inch round pieces
$^3/_4$ teaspoon salt
2 tablespoons coriander powder
1 tablespoon dry mango powder (amchur)
2 tablespoons fennel seeds, crushed

Method:

Heat oil in pan over medium-high heat. Add mustard seeds and turmeric powder. When seeds start to pop, add chili peppers. Stir for 2 minutes. Turn heat to medium. Add salt, coriander powder, dry mango powder and fennel seeds. Keep stirring for 2-3 minutes. Turn heat off.

Serving suggestion
Goes well with any meal or dal bati as a side dish.

Preferred kitchenware
• *Large non stick frying pan*

Papad Subzi

Rajasthani Papad Dish with Yogurt

Serves 4

Preparation time: 10 mins.
Cooking time: 15 mins.

Ingredients:

4 large Bikaneri papad*
4 tablespoons plain yogurt
$1^3/_4$ cups water
2 tablespoons oil
$^1/_2$ teaspoon cumin seeds
$^1/_2$ teaspoon turmeric powder
1 tablespoon coriander powder
$^1/_4$ teaspoon red chili powder
$^1/_4$ teaspoon salt
2 teaspoons dry mango powder (amchur)
$^1/_2$ teaspoon garam masala
1 tablespoon coriander, chopped

*Available in Indian grocery stores

Method:

Crush papad into small pieces (about $1-1^1/_2$ inch) by hand. Thoroughly mix yogurt and water making sure no lumps remain.

Heat oil in pan over medium-high heat. Add cumin seeds. When seeds start to pop, add turmeric powder, coriander powder and roast for 30 seconds. Add red chili powder and yogurt mix. Keep stirring until mixture comes to a boil.

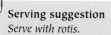*TLC Tip: Constant stirring is very important; otherwise yogurt will separate from mixture.*

Add salt, dry mango powder and papad. Let cook for 1 minute on low heat.

Turn heat off and add garam masala. Garnish with chopped coriander.

Serving suggestion
Serve with rotis.

Preferred kitchenware
• *$1^1/_2$ qt. saucepan with lid*

Rajma
Red Kidney Beans in Spicy Sauce
Serves 4

Preparation time: 9 hrs.
Cooking time: 45 mins.

Ingredients:
1 cup dried red kidney beans
2 $^3/_4$ cups water
1 teaspoon salt
$^1/_2$ teaspoon turmeric powder
$^3/_4$ cup precooked masala
See recipe on page 172
1 teaspoon red chili powder
$^1/_2$ teaspoon garam masala
2 tablespoons coriander, chopped

Method:
Wash and soak beans for 8 hours. Rinse and drain. Put beans, water, salt, and turmeric powder in pressure cooker on medium high heat. Close lid and put weight on. After pressure builds up, turn heat to medium-low and cook for 15 minutes. Turn off heat and leave covered for 15 minutes. Put pressure cooker under cold running water to reduce pressure and open lid. Add precooked masala and stir. Add red chili powder and cook for about 15 minutes on medium-low heat without pressure, stirring occasionally. Add garam masala, stir, turn heat off, and cover.

Before serving, garnish with chopped coriander.

☙ *TLC Tip: Canned kidney beans can be used in this recipe.*
☙ *TLC Tip: Rajma can be frozen in air tight containers for future use.*

Serving suggestion
Goes well with basmati rice and cucumber raita.

Preferred kitchenware
• *4 qt. steel pressure cooker*

Sag Paneer
Spinach and Cheese with Tomatoes
Serves 4

Preparation time: 1 hr.
Cooking time: 20 mins.

Ingredients:
10 ounces frozen chopped spinach, thawed
$1^1/_4$ cups water
$^3/_4$ cup precooked masala
See recipe on page 172
1 cup paneer cubes, fried
See recipe on page 171
$^1/_2$ teaspoon salt
$^1/_4$ teaspoon garam masala

Method:
Grind spinach with water in blender. Put saucepan on medium-high heat. Add spinach, precooked masala, paneer and salt. Stir, cover and cook for 2 minutes. Reduce heat to medium-low and cook for 10 minutes, stirring occasionally. Add garam masala, stir and turn heat off.

☙ *TLC Tip: Sag Paneer freezes well and you can make extra and freeze in air tight containers for future use.*

Serving suggestion
Serve this party dish with nan.

Preferred kitchenware
- *2 qt. saucepan*
- *Blender*

Sarson ka Sag

Mustard Greens from the Punjab

Serves 4

Preparation time: 1 hr.
Cooking time: 25 mins.

Ingredients:

5 ounces frozen mustard greens, thawed
5 ounces frozen spinach, thawed
5 ounces frozen broccoli, thawed
1 small green chili
$^1/_2$ inch ginger, fresh, peeled and cut into pieces
$1^1/_4$ cups water (for grinding)
$^3/_4$ teaspoon salt
$1^1/_2$ tablespoons corn flour
3 tablespoons water (for mixing corn flour)
For tempering:
$1^1/_2$ tablespoons oil
$^1/_4$ teaspoon cumin seeds
Pinch of asafetida
1 medium onion, chopped
$^1/_8$ stick butter
$^1/_2$ teaspoon garam masala

Serving suggestion
*Serve with makki ki roti (corn rotis)
and salty lassi.*

Preferred kitchenware
- *2 qt. saucepan*
- *Small frying pan*
- *Blender*

Method:

Grind vegetables including ginger and green chili with water in blender to a smooth texture.

Place saucepan on medium heat, add ground vegetable mixture and salt. Mix corn flour with 3 tablespoons of water and add to saucepan. Stir. Reduce heat to low, cover and cook for 15-20 minutes. Stir occasionally while cooking.

Heat oil in small frying pan. Add cumin seeds and asafetida. Cook on medium heat until seeds starts to pop. Add onions and sauté, stirring constantly, until lightly brown. Add contents of frying pan into saucepan containing vegetables. Finally, add butter and garam masala. Cook for another 2 minutes.

Shahi Paneer

'Royal' Cheese in Cream Sauce

Serves 4

Preparation time: 30 mins.
Cooking time: 20 mins.

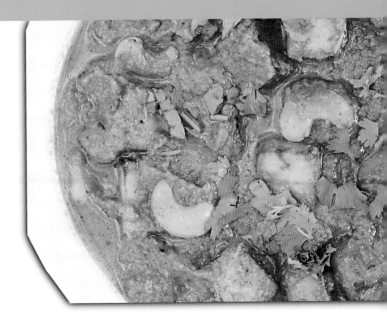

Ingredients:

3 medium tomatoes, cut into cubes
$1/_2$ cup yogurt
2 medium onions, chopped
1 one-inch piece ginger
1 medium green chili
4 tablespoons oil
2 black cardamoms
1 stick cinnamon (2 inch long)
4 bay leaves
1 teaspoon salt
$1/_2$ teaspoon turmeric powder
$1/_2$ teaspoon red chili powder
4 teaspoons coriander powder
$1/_2$ cup water
2 cups paneer, cubes, fried
See recipe on page 171
$1/_8$ cup coconut powder
$1/_8$ cup cashew nuts, fried
1 teaspoon garam masala
1 teaspoon sugar
$1/_4$ cup light cream
2 tablespoons coriander, chopped

> **Serving suggestion**
> *This party dish goes well with boondi raita, gobhi alu and nan/tandoori roti/parantha.*

> **Preferred kitchenware**
> • *Blender*
> • *2 qt. saucepan*

Method:

Blend tomatoes and yogurt in blender and set aside. Blend onion, ginger and green chili to a fine paste. Heat oil in pan on medium heat. Add cardamom, cinnamon and bay leaves. When leaves turn light brown, add onion, chili and ginger paste. Sauté until light brown. Add all other spices except garam masala. Sauté for 2 minutes. Add yogurt and tomato mixture. Add water. When mixture comes to a boil, cover and cook for 5-7 minutes. Add fried paneer cubes, coconut and cashew nuts. Reduce heat to low and cook for 5-7 minutes partially covered, stirring occasionally. Add garam masala, sugar and cream. Cook for 3-4 minutes. Turn heat off and garnish with chopped coriander.

Sev Sabzi
Spicy Apple without Sauce
Serves 4

Preparation time: 10 mins.
Cooking time: 15 mins.

Ingredients:

2 tablespoons oil
$1/2$ teaspoon cumin seeds
$1/2$ teaspoon mustard seeds
$1/2$ teaspoon turmeric powder
Pinch of asafetida
4 medium Granny Smith apples, cut in to long slices
1 teaspoon salt
2 green chilies slit in to long slices
1 teaspoon dry mango powder (amchur)
$1/2$ teaspoon red chili powder
$1/2$ teaspoon garam masala
1 teaspoon sugar

Method:

Heat oil in pan over medium high heat. Add cumin seeds, mustard seeds, turmeric powder and asafetida. When cumin seeds start to pop, add apple slices, salt and green chilies. Stir and reduce heat to medium. Cook covered for 8-10 minutes stirring occasionally. Add dry mango powder, chili powder, garam masala and sugar. Stir and turn heat off.

Serving suggestion
Serve with rotis and karhi.

Preferred kitchenware
• *Nonstick frying pan with lid*

Sukhe Alu
Spicy Potato without Sauce
Serves 4

Preparation time: 30 mins.
Cooking time: 25 mins.

Ingredients:

3 tablespoons oil
$^1/_4$ teaspoon cumin seeds
Pinch of asafetida
$^1/_4$ teaspoon turmeric powder
6 medium potatoes, boiled, peeled, crushed or cut into $^3/_4$ inch pieces
$^3/_4$ teaspoon salt
1 teaspoon green chilies, chopped
$^3/_4$ teaspoon red chili powder
3 teaspoons coriander powder
$1^1/_4$ teaspoons dry mango powder (amchur)
2 tablespoons coriander, chopped

Method:

Heat oil in pan over medium heat. Add cumin seeds, asafetida, and turmeric powder. When cumin seeds start to pop, add potatoes, salt, green chili and other spices. Stir and reduce heat to low. Cook uncovered for 5 to 7 minutes stirring occasionally. Turn heat off.
Garnish with chopped coriander.

Serving suggestion
Serve with pooris and pickles. In India, people usually take pooris and sukhe alu to picnics.

Preferred kitchenware
- *Nonstick frying pan with lid*
- *2 qt. Sauce pan for boiling*

Sukhi Matar
Peas without Sauce
Serves 4

Preparation time: 1 hr.
Cooking time: 20 mins.

Ingredients:
2 tablespoons oil
Pinch of asafetida
$1^1/_2$ inch piece ginger, cut into
thin slices (optional)
16 ounces frozen peas, thawed (fresh peas taste better)
1/2 teaspoon salt
1/2 teaspoon garam masala
1/2 teaspoon black pepper
1 teaspoon sugar
2 tablespoons coriander, chopped

Method:
Heat oil in pan on medium heat. Add asafetida and ginger. Stir in peas and salt. Cover and reduce heat to medium-low and cook for 10-15 minutes, stirring occasionally. Add garam masala, black pepper and sugar. Reduce heat to low. Cover and let cook for 5 minutes.
Garnish with chopped coriander before serving.

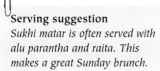

Serving suggestion
Sukhi matar is often served with alu parantha and raita. This makes a great Sunday brunch.

Preferred kitchenware
• *Non-stick frying pan with lid*

Talasani
Konkani Style Green Beans with Garlic
Serves 4

Preparation time: 15 mins.
Cooking time: 15 mins.

Ingredients:
1 pound fresh green beans
3 tablespoons oil
$^1/_2$ teaspoon mustard seeds
2 cloves garlic, chopped
1 teaspoon urad dal
$^1/_2$ teaspoon salt
$^1/_4$ teaspoon turmeric powder
$^1/_2$ teaspoon red chili powder

Method:
Wash beans, cut two ends off and break in half.
Heat oil in pan on medium-high heat. Add mustard
seeds. When seeds start to pop, add garlic and
dal. When dal turns light brown, add beans, and
remaining spices. Stir and cover, reducing heat to
medium-low. Stir a few more times and cook until
beans are soft yet crunchy.

Serving suggestion
Tastes good with plain paranthas.

Preferred kitchenware
Non-stick frying pan

Upkari
Konkani Style Green Beans with Coconut
Serves 4

Preparation time: 15 mins.
Cooking time: 15 mins.

Ingredients:
1 pound fresh green beans
3 tablespoons oil
$1/_2$ teaspoon mustard seeds
1 teaspoon urad dal
$1/_2$ teaspoon salt
$1/_4$ teaspoon turmeric powder
$1/_2$ teaspoon red chili powder
2 tablespoons water
1 teaspoon sugar or
1 small piece gud (unrefined raw sugar piece)
2 tablespoons coconut, grated (unsweetened)

Method:
Wash beans. Discard the two ends. Cut into $1/_4$ inch pieces.
Heat oil in pan on medium-high heat. Add mustard seeds. When seeds start to pop, add dal. When dal turns light brown, add beans and remaining spices. Stir and add water. Cover and reduce heat to medium-low. Stir a few more times and cook till beans are soft yet crunchy. Add sugar or gud and coconut and cook for another 2 minutes.

Serving suggestion
Tastes good with plain paranthas.

Preferred kitchenware
• *Nonstick frying pan*

Dals and Dal Variants

Arhar Dal

aka Toor Dal

Serves 4

Preparation time: 1hr.
Cooking time: 1hr.

Ingredients:

1 cup arhar dal
$2^1/_2$ cups water
1 teaspoon salt
$^1/_4$ teaspoon turmeric powder
For tempering:
1 tablespoon of ghee/butter/oil
$^1/_4$ teaspoon cumin seeds
Pinch of asafetida
$^1/_4$ teaspoon red chili powder

Method:

Thoroughly wash and soak dal for 1 hour in warm water. Drain and put in saucepan. Add water, salt and turmeric powder. Cook on high heat until it starts to boil. Turn heat to low, cover and allow it to simmer for 40-45 minutes stirring several times. When dal is tender and has mixed well with water, remove from stove and cover.

Tempering: Heat oil/ghee/butter in small frying pan. Add cumin seeds and asafetida. When cumin seeds start to pop or become golden brown, add red chili powder and immediately pour over dal and mix.

☙ *TLC Tip: Red chili powder burns fast, therefore remember to turnoff stove immediately after adding it.*

☙ *TLC Tip: Asafetida is always added to dal because it neutralizes the gassiness of lentils and beans.*

Serving suggestion
This dal is usually eaten with basmati rice.

Preferred kitchenware
- $1^1/_2$ *qt. saucepan with lid*
- *Small frying pan*

Chhilka Mung Dal
Split Unshelled Mung
Serves 4

Preparation time: 1 hr.
Cooking time: 35 mins.

Ingredients:
1 cup split mung dal
$3^1/_2$ cups water
1 teaspoon salt
$^1/_2$ teaspoon turmeric powder
1 medium onion, finely chopped
2 medium tomatoes, finely chopped
1 tablespoon ginger, chopped
1 tablespoon green chili, chopped
3 tablespoons lemon juice
$^1/_2$ teaspoon garam masala
2 tablespoons coriander, chopped
For tempering:
2 tablespoons oil or ghee
$^1/_2$ teaspoon cumin seeds
Pinch of asafetida
$^1/_4$ teaspoon red chili powder

Method:
Rinse and soak dal in $3^1/_2$ cups of water for 1 hour. Place pan over high heat. Put dal and water in to saucepan. Add, salt, turmeric powder, onions, tomatoes, ginger and green chili. When mixture comes to boil, turn heat to low. Cover and allow to simmer for 20-25 minutes. Stir several times. When dal has mixed with water, add lemon juice and garam masala. Garnish with chopped coriander.
Tempering: In small frying pan heat ghee or oil. Add cumin seeds and asafetida. When cumin seeds start to pop or become golden brown, add red chili powder and immediately pour into dal and mix.
❦ *TLC Tip: Red chili powder burns fast, therefore turn off stove immediately after adding it.*
❦ *TLC Tip: Asafetida is added to dal because it neutralizes gassiness of lentils and beans.*

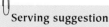

Serving suggestion
This dal is usually served with basmati rice, rotis, and any green vegetable.

Preferred kitchenware
- *$1^1/_2$ qt. saucepan with lid*
- *Small frying pan*

Dal Makhani
Dal Cooked with Butter
Serves 4

Preparation time: 30 mins.
Cooking time: 1 hr. 20 mins.

Ingredients:

1 cup whole urad
4 cups water
$^3/_4$ teaspoon salt
$^1/_4$ teaspoon turmeric powder
1 tablespoon oil
8 oz. sour cream
$^1/_4$ stick butter
$^3/_4$ cup precooked masala
See recipe on page 172
1 teaspoon red chili powder
$^1/_2$ teaspoon garam masala
2 tablespoons coriander, chopped

Method:

Wash and soak dal for 30 minutes in warm water. Rinse and drain. Put dal in pressure cooker, adding water, salt, turmeric powder and oil on medium-high heat. Close lid and put weight on. After pressure builds up, turn heat to medium- low and cook for 15 minutes or until dal gets soft but not mushy. Turn off heat and leave it covered for 5 minutes. Put pressure cooker under cold running water to reduce pressure and open lid. Put pressure cooker back on stove on medium-low heat. Add sour cream, butter and stir. Cook half covered for 30 minutes.

Add precooked masala and stir. Add red chili powder and cook for about 30 minutes on low heat, stirring occasionally. Add garam masala, stir and turn heat off. Garnish with chopped coriander.

❦ *TLC Tip: Since Dal Makhani is elaborate to prepare, make extra and freeze in air tight containers for future use.*

Serving suggestion
This is a party dal that can be eaten with rice or any kind of Indian bread.

Preferred kitchenware
• *4 qt. steel pressure cooker*

Panchmel Dal

Mixed Dal

Serves 4

Preparation time: 1 hr.
Cooking time: 50 mins.

Ingredients:

$^1/_2$ cup arhar dal
$^1/_8$ cup each urad, mung, chana (gram),
and masoor (lentil) dal (for a total of $^1/_2$ cup)
$2^1/_2$ cups water
1 teaspoon salt
$^1/_4$ teaspoon turmeric powder
2 tablespoons fresh lemon juice
For tempering:
2 tablespoons oil or ghee
$^1/_2$ teaspoon cumin seeds
$^1/_2$ teaspoon mustard seeds
Pinch of asafetida
$^1/_4$ teaspoon red chili powder
2 tablespoons coriander, chopped

Method:

Rinse and soak dals in warm water for 1 hour. Drain. Place pan on high heat, add dal, water, salt and turmeric powder. Stir. When mixture comes to a boil, reduce heat to low and cover pan, leaving a small opening between pan and lid. Stir occasionally. Cook for 40-45 minutes until dal gets soft. Mix well and add lemon juice. Heat oil in frying pan over medium heat. Add cumin seeds, mustard seeds and asafetida. Stir until the seeds start to pop. Add red chili powder.

TLC Tip: Red chili powder burns fast, therefore remember to turn off stove immediately after adding it.

Add this mixture to dal. Finally, add chopped coriander.

Serving suggestion
This dal goes well with bati. Add fresh lemon juice to enhance flavor.

Preferred kitchenware
• *$1^1/_2$ qt. saucepan with lid*
• *Small frying pan*

Sabut Masoor Dal Amti
Sweet and Sour Dal from Mumbai
Serves 4

Preparation time: 1 hr.
Cooking time: 40 mins.

Ingredients:

1 cup whole lentil (masoor) dal (arhar dal can be substituted)
1 teaspoon salt
2 teaspoons sugar or gud (unrefined sugar pieces)
$1/2$ teaspoon turmeric powder
$3^1/_2$ cups water
2 tablespoons of ghee or melted butter
$1/2$ teaspoon cumin seeds
$1/2$ teaspoon mustard seeds
1 medium onion, chopped
2 cloves of garlic, chopped
2 medium tomatoes, chopped
1 teaspoon Amti powder*
2 tablespoons green corainder, chopped

* For Amti powder, roast and grind:
6 teaspoons coriander seeds
3 teaspoons cumin seeds
1 teaspoon black cumin seeds
4 cloves
$1/2$ inch cinnamon stick

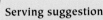

Serving suggestion
This dal goes well with basmati rice and green vegetables.

Preferred kitchenware
- *4 qt. pressure cooker*
- *Medium frying pan*

Method:

Wash and soak dal in warm water for 1 hour and drain. Add dal, salt, sugar, turmeric powder and water in pressure cooker on medium high heat. Close lid and put weight on. When the pressure builds up and cooker whistles, turn heat to low and cook for 15 minutes. Remove from heat and wait until steam is dissipated. Carefully remove lid from pressure cooker. Heat ghee in small frying pan. Add cumin and mustard seeds. After mustard seeds start to pop, add onions and garlic. When onions turn light brown, add tomatoes. When tomatoes become soft, add amti powder and sauté for 1 minute. Pour the whole sizzling mixture into dal and stir. Garnish with chopped corainder.

❦ *TLC Tip: Left over Amti can be stored in an airtight plastic container in freezer.*

Sabut Mung or Masoor Dal

Whole Mung or Lentil Dal
Serves 4

Preparation time: 1 hr.
Cooking time: 40 mins.

Ingredients:

1 cup whole mung or lentil (masoor)
1 teaspoon salt
$^1/_2$ teaspoon turmeric powder
4 cups water
2 tablespoons lemon juice
For tempering:
2 tablespoons oil or ghee
$^1/_2$ teaspoon cumin seeds
Pinch of asafetida
$^1/_4$ teaspoon red chili powder
2 tablespoons coriander, chopped

Method:

Wash and soak dal for 1 hour. Drain. Put dal, salt, turmeric powder and water in pressure cooker on medium high heat. Close lid and put weight on. When the pressure builds up and cooker whistles, turn heat to low and cook for 15 minutes. Remove from heat and let sit until steam dissipates. Carefully remove lid from pressure cooker, add lemon juice and mix.

Tempering: Heat ghee or oil in a small frying pan. Add cumin seeds and asafetida. When cumin seeds turn golden brown, add red chili powder and immediately pour into dal. Garnish with chopped coriander.

🌿 *TLC Tip: Red chili powder burns fast, therefore remember to turn off stove immediately after adding it.*

Serving suggestion
This dal goes well with Basmati rice and a green vegetable.

Preferred kitchenware
• *4 qt. steel pressure cooker*
• *Very small frying pan*

Sambhar

South Indian Dal Preparation
Serves 4

Preparation time: 1 hr.
Cooking time: 25 mins.

Ingredients:

1 cup arhar dal
4 cups water
1 teaspoon salt
$^1/_2$ teaspoon turmeric powder
$^1/_4$ cup green beans, cut into small pieces
1 carrot, cut into small pieces
3 tablespoons oil
1 teaspoon mustard seeds
1 large onion, chopped
6-8 pieces curry leaves
1 large tomato, chopped
$2^1/_2$ teaspoons Sambhar powder *
1 teaspoon tamarind (imli) paste
2 tablespoons coriander, chopped

* Available at Indian Grocery Stores
  Recipe page 175

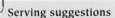

Serving suggestions
Serve with idlis and coconut chutney.
A favorite dish for brunch.

Preferred kitchenware
- *4 qt. pressure cooker*
- *Medium nonstick frying pan*

Method:

Wash and soak dal in warm water for 1 hour and drain. Put water, salt, turmeric powder, green beans, carrots and dal in pressure cooker on medium high heat. Close lid and put weight on. When the pressure builds up and cooker whistles, turn heat off and set aside for 10-15 minutes. When steam dissipates, carefully remove lid from pressure cooker. Heat oil in small frying pan on medium heat. Add mustard seeds. When seeds start to pop, add onions and curry leaves. Sauté until onions turn golden brown. Add tomatoes and cook till soft. Add sambhar powder and sauté a few seconds more. Add this mixture to dal.

In the same pan, add $^1/_4$ cup water and tamarind paste and cook until they blend well. Pour into dal and stir. Garnish with chopped coriander.

Urad Dal

Serves 4

Preparation time: 1 hr.
Cooking time: 45 mins.

Ingredients:

1 cup urad dal
$4^1/_2$ cups water
1 teaspoon salt
$^1/_4$ teaspoon turmeric powder
$^1/_4$ teaspoon dry ginger powder (optional)
For tempering:
2 tablespoons oil or ghee
Pinch of asafetida
$^1/_4$ teaspoon red chili powder

Method:

Thoroughly rinse and soak dal in warm water for 1 hour. Drain. Put pan on high heat, add dal, water, salt and turmeric powder. Stir. When mixture comes to a boil, reduce heat to low and cover, leaving a small opening between pan and lid. Stir occasionally. Cook for 30-35 minutes until dal gets tender and mixes with water. Add ginger powder.

Tempering: Heat oil or ghee in small frying pan. Add asafetida and chili powder. Add this mixture to dal.

🌶 *TLC Tip: Red chili powder burns fast, therefore remember to turn off stove immediately after adding it.*

Serving suggestion
Serve with rotis. Mint and coriander chutney goes well with it. Suggested vegetable: Bhindi masala.

Preferred kitchenware
- $1^1/_2$ qt. saucepan with lid
- *Very small frying pan*

Gatte

Rolled Gram Flour Pieces in Yogurt Sauce
Serves 4

Preparation time: 15 mins.
Cooking time: 40 mins.

Ingredients:

Gatte (Chunks):
$1^1/_2$ cups gram flour (besan)
$^1/_4$ teaspoon salt
$^1/_4$ teaspoon turmeric powder
$^1/_4$ teaspoon red chili powder
$^1/_2$ teaspoon garam masala
4 tablespoons oil
3 tablespoons plain yogurt
2 tablespoons water (for mixing)
3 $^1/_2$ cups water (for boiling)
Sauce:
$^3/_4$ cup plain yogurt
$1^1/_2$ cups water (left over from boiling gatte)
2 tablespoons oil
$^1/_2$ teaspoon turmeric powder
$^1/_2$ teaspoon red chili powder
$^1/_2$ teaspoon paprika (for color)
$^3/_4$ teaspoon salt
$^1/_4$ teaspoon garam masala
2 tablespoons coriander, chopped

Method:

Gatte: Mix gram flour, salt, turmeric powder, red chili powder, garam masala and oil. Add yogurt and water and make into a dough.
🌢 *TLC Tip: This will stick to hands. Peel off with the back of a knife. Keeping hands wet will minimize this.*
Boil water on high heat. With moistened hands, roll dough into strips about the length and diameter of hot dog. Put rolls into boiling water and reduce heat to medium. Do not cover. Boil for 10 minutes. Remove rolls. Cool and cut into pieces about $^1/_2$ inch long. Save this water for sauce.
Sauce: Whisk yogurt until smooth (no lumps) and add $1^1/_2$ cups remaining water (used for boiling) from above and mix. Heat oil in pan on medium-high heat. Add turmeric powder, red chili powder, paprika and yogurt mixture. Keep stirring until mixture boils. Add salt, garam masala and gatte. Turn heat to low and cook for 10 minutes, partially covered, stirring occasionally. Before serving, garnish with chopped coriander.

Serving Suggestions
This Rajasthani preparation is great with dal and bati or roti with side vegetables.

Preferred kitchenware
• *3 qt. covered saucepan*
• *Medium sized mixing bowl*

Pakoda Karhi or Plain Karhi
(For Plain Karhi, Omit Pakoda)
Serves 4

Preparation time: 25 mins.
Cooking time: 30 mins.

Ingredients:

Pakoda:
$1/_2$ cup gram flour (besan)
$1/_3$ cup water
$1/_4$ teaspoon salt
$1/_4$ teaspoon red chili powder
2 cups oil (for frying)
Pinch of baking soda

Karhi:
$1/_4$ cup gram flour (besan)
$1^1/_4$ cups plain yogurt*
2 cups water
2 tablespoons oil
$1/_2$ teaspoon mustard seeds
$1/_2$ teaspoon turmeric powder
4-5 curry leaves (optional)
$1/_2$ teaspoon red chili powder
$1^1/_4$ teaspoons salt
$1/_4$ teaspoon garam masala

*TLC Tip: The yogurt should be sour. You can leave it out for 4-5 hours. Or you can add a tablespoon of lemon juice after the karhi has cooked and stir.

Method:

Pakodas: Mix gram flour with water, salt and red chili powder. Whisk until no lumps remain and set aside for 10 minutes.

Heat oil in kadhai on medium-high. While oil is getting hot, add baking soda to mixture.

🍎 *TLC Tip: To test if temperature of oil is correct for frying; put a small drop of pakoda mixture in. If it rises rapidly, oil is ready. If it stays at bottom or rises very slowly, wait and try again.*

Remove test pieces from oil before starting to fry. Drop by spoonfuls, about 1 teaspoonful of mixture at a time.

Serving suggestions
Serve with Basmati rice and papad.

Preferred kitchenware
- *2 qt. saucepan with lid and handle*
- *Two 2 qt. mixing bowls*
- *Kadhai or deep frying pan*
- *Jharar (slotted spoon)*

Repeat until 10-12 pakodas are in oil.

☙ *TLC Tip: Do not drop from a height of more than 1 inch or hot oil will splatter and may burn hands.*

Turn pakodas several times until golden brown. Drain oil from pakodas by raising spatula and tapping it very lightly against the side of kadhai to shake off excess oil. Place pakodas on paper towel to absorb remaining oil. Repeat until entire mixture is used.

☙ *TLC Tip: If at anytime oil starts to smoke, or pakodas turn black, oil is too hot. Reduce heat and wait until temperature is correct again.*

Karhi: Whisk gram flour, yogurt and water until smooth and no lumps remains. Heat oil in saucepan on medium-high heat. Add mustard seeds. When seeds start to pop, add turmeric powder, curry leaves, red chili powder and karhi mixture, stirring constantly until it boils. Add salt, pakodas, garam masala, and cook for 2 minutes. Reduce heat to low, and let cook for 10 minutes, stirring slowly once or twice (so as not to break pakodas).

☙ *TLC Tip: Pakodas can be made ahead of time and frozen in air tight containers or freezer bags for future use.*

! Caution: Never leave oil unattended over a stove. If overheated, the oil can catch fire, causing serious injury!

! Caution: Use extreme care when deep frying. Due to a combination of factors, the object being fried may burst causing the hot oil to spatter. Some of the causes can be adding too much water, the oil being too hot, or the ingredients being old stock due to poor turnover in the store. It is always advisable to stand a fair distance away from the stove until you have made sure this is not happening. Also, you can hold a spatter screen as a safe guard.

For help: www.momsindiancooking.com

Palak Karhi
Karhi with Spinach
Serves 4

Preparation time: 1 hr.
Cooking time: 40 mins.

Ingredients:

$1/4$ cup gram flour (besan)
$1^1/_4$ cups plain yogurt*
2 cups water
3 tablespoons oil
$1/4$ teaspoon cumin seeds
$1/4$ teaspoon mustard seeds
Pinch of asafetida
1 small onion, sliced
10 oz frozen chopped spinach,
thawed (or 1 small fresh bunch)
$1/2$ teaspoon turmeric powder
$1/2$ teaspoon red chili powder
$1/2$ teaspoon garam masala
1 teaspoon salt

*TLC Tip: The yogurt should be sour. You can leave it out for 4-5 hours. Or you can add a tablespoon of lemon juice after the karhi has cooked and stir.

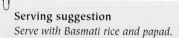

Serving suggestion
Serve with Basmati rice and papad.

Preferred kitchenware
• *2 qt. saucepan with handle*
• *2 qt. mixing bowl*

Method:

Whisk gram flour, yogurt and water until smooth (no lumps). Heat oil in pan on medium heat. Add cumin seeds, mustard seeds and asafetida. When seeds start to pop, add onions stirring until lightly browned. Add spinach and cook for 5 minutes, stirring continuously. Add turmeric powder, red chili powder, garam masala and cook for another minute. Add gram flour and yogurt mixture. Keep stirring until it starts to boil. Reduce heat to low and add salt. Cook for 25 minutes partially covered, stirring occasionally.

Mangochi

North Indian Mung Dal Pakodas in Yogurt Sauce

Serves 4

Preparation time: 3 hrs 30 mins.
Cooking time: 1 hr.

Ingredients:

Pakoda:
1 cup mung dal
$^1/_2$ cup water
$^1/_2$ teaspoon salt
2 cups oil (for frying)
Sauce:
1$^1/_2$ cups plain yogurt*
4 cups water
2 tablespoons oil
$^1/_2$ teaspoon cumin seeds
6 cloves
$^1/_2$ teaspoon turmeric powder
$^1/_2$ teaspoon red chili powder
1 teaspoon salt
$^1/_4$ teaspoon garam masala

Method:

Pakodas: Soak dal in water for 3 hours. Drain well and grind in blender with half a cup of water to a fine texture. Add salt to the mixture.
Put oil in kadhai on medium-high heat.
☙ *TLC Tip: To test temperature, put a small drop of pakoda mix in. If it rises rapidly, oil is ready. If it stays at bottom or rises slowly, try again.*
Remove test pieces from oil before starting to fry.

*TLC Tip: The yogurt should be sour. You can leave it out for 4-5 hours. Or you can add a table spoon of lemon juice after the Mangochi has cooked.

❗ Caution: Use extreme care when deep frying. Due to a combination of factors, the object being fried may burst causing the hot oil to spatter. Some of the causes can be adding too much water, the oil being too hot, or the ingredients being old stock due to poor turnover in the store. It is always advisable to stand a fair distance away from the stove until you have made sure this is not happening. Also, you can hold a spatter screen as a safe guard.

Drop pakoda mix one teaspoonful at a time into oil. Repeat continuously until about 10-12 pakodas are in oil.

🌿 *TLC Tip: Do not drop from a height of more than 1 inch or hot oil will splatter and may burn your hand.*

Turn pakodas several times until golden brown. Drain oil from pakodas by raising spatula and tapping it against the side of kadhai very lighty to shake off excess oil. Place pakodas on paper towel over a plate to absorb remaining oil. Repeat until all mixture is used.

🌿*TLC Tip: If at anytime oil starts to smoke, or pakodas start to turn black, oil is too hot. Reduce heat and wait until temperature is right again.*

Soak pakodas in water for 30 minutes. Gently press pakodas between palms and squeeze to remove excess water.

Sauce: Whisk yogurt with 4 cups of water until no lumps remain. Heat oil in saucepan on medium-high heat and add cumin seeds and cloves. When seeds start to pop, add turmeric powder, red chili powder, and yogurt mixture. Keep stirring until mixture comes to a boil. Add pakodas.

🌿*TLC Tip: Constant stirring is very important, otherwise yogurt will separate from mixture.*

Add salt, garam masala and reduce heat to low and cook for another 6 minutes.

❗ Caution: Never leave oil unattended over a stove. If overheated, the oil can catch fire, causing serious injury

For help: www.momsindiancooking.com

Serving suggestion
Serve with roti and green vegetable.

Preferred kitchenware
- *3 qt. saucepan with lid and handle*
- *Two 2 qt. mixing bowls*
- *Kadhai or deep frying pan*
- *Jharar (slotted spoon)*
- *Blender*

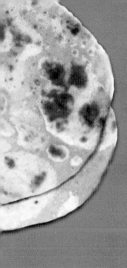

Breads and Bread Variants

Bati

Rajasthani Oven Roasted Dough Balls
Makes 8-9 batis

Preparation time: 2 hrs 15 mins.
Cooking time: 1hr.

Ingredients:

2 cups whole wheat flour
1 teaspoon salt
4 tablespoons oil
3 tablespoons plain yogurt
$\frac{1}{2}$ cup warm water
$\frac{1}{4}$ cup ghee, melted

Serving suggestion
Serve hot with mixed dal and gatte.
Green chutney and sliced onions may
be served as accompaniments. Also
serve Choorme ke Laddoo for dessert
along with bati.

Preferred kitchenware
• *2 qt. mixing bowl*

Method:

Combine flour, salt, oil in bowl and mix well. Add yogurt and water and knead dough until it no longer sticks to bowl.

☙ *TLC Tip: It may help to put some oil on your hands to prevent dough from sticking to fingers.*

Cover and set aside for 2 hours. Knead dough again and make 8 to 9 balls. Lightly press dough between your hands to flatten slightly. Preheat oven to 300ºF. Spread aluminum foil on middle rack and place batis on it. Cook for 20 minutes, turn batis and raise temperature to 400ºF. Cook for 30 minutes until golden brown, turning once or twice in between. Remove from oven; crush very gently to slightly crack the top. Dip in ghee draining excess back into cup.

Bhature

All Purpose Flour Fried Bread from the Punjab
Makes about 12

Preparation time: 4 hrs.
Cooking time: 5 mins. each

Ingredients:
1 teaspoon dry active yeast
3 cups all purpose flour (for dough)
1 teaspoon salt
6 ounces warm water
7 tablespoons plain yogurt
$1/_2$ cup all purpose flour (for rolling)
2-3 cups oil (for frying)

Method:
Dissolve yeast in 2 tablespoons of warm water. Mix well 3 cups of flour and salt in medium bowl. Mix water, yogurt and yeast and add this mixture to flour. Knead dough until it does not stick to bowl.
🍃 *TLC Tip: It may help to put some oil on your hands to prevent dough from sticking to fingers.*
Cover and set aside for 3 to 4 hours for dough to rise. Knead again and divide dough into 12 equal parts. Squeeze each portion between hands one at a time and make into balls. Lightly press between hands to flatten to 2 inch diameter.
🍃 *TLC Tip: Apply some dry flour, when required, to prevent from sticking to rolling pin and flour board.*
Roll out dough into about 5 inch diameter. Heat oil in kadhai over medium-high heat.
🍃 *TLC Tip: To test the temperature of oil, put a small drop of dough in. If it rises to the surface rapidly, it is ready. If it stays at the bottom or rises very slowly, wait and try again. Remove this test piece from oil before starting to fry.*
Fry one bhatura at a time.
🍃 *TLC Tip: Slide in from side-do not drop in middle. Splashed oil can cause serious burns.*
When one side becomes slightly brown, flip and fry other side. Drain excess oil and remove. Serve hot.

Serving suggestion
Serve with chhole and sliced onions in lemon juice.

Preferred kitchenware
- *2 qt. mixing bowl*
- *Flour board*
- *Rolling pin*
- *Kadhai or deep frying pan*
- *Jharar (slotted spoon)*

! **Caution: Never leave oil unattended over a stove. If overheated, the oil can catch fire, causing serious injury**

For help: www.momsindiancooking.com

Kachori

UP Style Stuffed Poori

Makes about 24

Preparation time: 9 hrs.
Cooking time: 5 mins. each

Ingredients:

Filling:
1 cup urad dal
2 tablespoons oil
Pinch of asafetida
1 teaspoon salt
$^1/_2$ teaspoon red chili powder
1 tablespoon dry mango powder (amchur)
$^1/_2$ teaspoon garam masala
2 teaspoons crushed fennel seeds
$^1/_2$ teaspoon ginger powder

3 cups whole wheat flour
$^1/_2$ teaspoon salt
3 tablespoons oil (for kneading dough)
10-11 ounces warm water (for kneading)
2-3 tablespoons oil (for rolling)
2-3 cups oil (for frying)

Method:

Thoroughly wash and soak dal in water for 8 hours. Drain and grind dal coarsely in food processor.

Heat 2 tablespoons of oil in frying pan on medium-high heat. Add asafetida and let cook for a few seconds. Add dal and rest of spices. Cook for 5 minutes, stirring continously. Remove from heat and let cool.

Mix well 3 cups of flour, salt and oil in bowl. Add water and knead dough until it does not stick to bowl any more.

🍃 *TLC Tip: It may help to put some oil on your hands to prevent dough from sticking to fingers.*

Cover and set aside for 15 minutes. Knead dough again, divide into 24 equal parts and shape each part into a ball. Lightly press ball between hands to flatten to 2 inch diameter. Grease rolling pin and flour board lightly with oil. Using moderate and uniform pressure, flatten ball with rolling pin to 3 inch diameter. Place 1 teaspoon of filling in middle. Fold over top of filling. Press edges together to seal. Again, flatten between palms to 2 inch diameter. Roll out with rolling pin to approximately 4 inch diameter.

🍃 *TLC Tip: While rolling, apply a little oil to dough 2-3 times to prevent sticking to flour board.*

Heat oil in kadhai on medium heat.

🍃 *TLC Tip: To test if temperature of oil is ready, put a small drop of dough in; if it rises to the surface fast, it is ready. If it stays at the bottom or rises very slowly, wait and try again. If it*

Remove the test piece from oil before starting to fry. Add 1 kachori at a time.

🍃 *TLC Tip: Slide kachori in from side. Do not drop in middle. Splashed oil can cause serious burns.*

It may help the puffing if kachori is pressed in oil with slotted spoon with very light pressure. When it has turned light brown, flip and fry the other side. Turn several times until golden brown on both sides. Drain excess oil and remove. Serve hot or stack and reheat in oven before serving.

Serving suggestion
Serve with chatpate alu. To serve later, wrap in aluminum foil and warm in hot oven for a few minutes.

Preferred kitchenware
- *Nonstick frying pan*
- *Flour board*
- *Food processor*
- *Jharar (slotted spoon)*
- *2 qt. mixing bowl*
- *Rolling pin*
- *Kadhai or deep frying pan*

❗**Caution: Never leave oil unattended over a stove. If overheated, the oil can catch fire, causing serious injury**

For help: www.momsindiancooking.com

Makki ki Roti

Roasted Corn Flour Bread from the Punjab
Makes about 10

Preparation time: 40 mins.
Cooking time: 5 mins. each

Ingredients:

3 cups corn flour (for dough)
$1/2$ teaspoon salt
2 cups warm water (for kneading)
$1/2$ cup whole wheat flour (for rolling)
Butter as needed

Method:

Mix flour and salt. Add a little water at a time and knead dough until it does not stick to bowl.

🌿 *TLC Tip: It may help to put some oil on your hands to prevent dough from sticking to fingers.*

Cover and set aside for 30 minutes. Knead dough again and make 10 equal balls. This dough is hard to handle without breaking apart. To help roll dough without breaking, spread one layer of plastic wrap on flour board. Lightly sprinkle with wheat flour. Press ball of dough between hands and flatten into 2 inch diameter. Place on plastic wrap sprinkled with flour. Sprinkle top of dough with some more wheat flour. Put another layer of plastic wrap on top. Flatten out with rolling pin using moderate and uniform pressure to 4 inches diameter.

Heat tawa for 2 to 3 minutes over medium heat. Turn on additional burner on medium heat (if electric, place cake rack over it). Remove top sheet of plastic. Carefully remove roti from bottom layer of plastic wrap and place on tawa. Wait until very small bubbles appear on surface. Turn it over and cook other side until brown spots appear. Using tongs, pick up roti and place it on the other burner, flipping it in the process. When it has turned golden brown, turn and cook other side for a few seconds. Remove from heat. Apply butter on one side.

🌿 *TLC Tip: For the beginners, it may be advisable to remove tawa from burner to prevent it from over heating while the roti is cooking on open fire. However, make sure it is reheated when you are ready for next roti. Experienced cooks do not need to do this.*

Serving suggestion
Serve hot with sarson ka sag and salty lassi, gud (unrefined sugar pieces) optional.

Preferred kitchenware
- *Saran wrap or other plastic wrap*
- *2 qt. mixing bowl*
- *Flour board*
- *Rolling pin*
- *Tawa or non stick frying pan*
- *Tongs*
- *Round cake-cooling rack (not needed for gas stoves)*

For help: www.momsindiancooking.com

Nan
Punjabi Oven Roasted Bread
Makes about 8

Preparation time: 4 hrs.
Cooking time: 5 mins per batch.

Ingredients:
3 cups all purpose flour (for dough)
1 teaspoon salt
$^1/_2$ teaspoon baking soda
4 teaspoons oil
6 ounces warm water
1 teaspoon dry active yeast, dissolved
in 2 tablespoons of warm water
7 tablespoons yogurt
$^1/_2$ cup all purpose flour (for rolling)
1 teaspoon Kalonji (onion seed) (optional)
1 teaspoon Khas Khas (poppy seeds) (optional)
Butter as needed (optional)

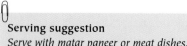

Serving suggestion
Serve with matar paneer or meat dishes.

Preferred kitchenware
- *2 qt. Mixing bowl*
- *Small mixing bowl*
- *Flour board*
- *Rolling pin*
- *Aluminum foil*

For help: www.momsindiancooking.com

Method:
Mix well 3 cups of flour, salt, baking soda and oil in 2 qt. bowl. Mix water, yeast and yogurt in small bowl. Add to flour and knead dough until it does not stick to the bowl.

TLC Tip: It may help to put some oil on your hands to prevent dough from sticking to fingers.

Cover and set aside for 3 to 4 hours for dough to rise. Knead again and divide into 8 equal parts. Shape each part into ball. Lightly press between hands to flatten to 2 inch diameter. Apply some dry flour as required (2 to 3 times) to prevent dough from sticking to rolling pin and flour board. Flatten out with rolling pin with moderate and uniform pressure to about 5 by 3 inch oblong shape. Sprinkle with onion and poppy seeds, and press lightly with hands.

Preheat oven on broil setting. Spread aluminum foil on top rack and place 4 nans at a time on it. When puffed and golden brown, flip and bake other side. Remove and apply butter on one side (optional). Serve hot.

Alu Parantha

North Indian Shallow Fried Bread
Filled with Potato
Makes about 10

Preparation time: 1 hr.
Cooking time: 3 mins. each

Ingredients:

2 cups whole wheat flour (for dough)
$^1/_2$ teaspoon salt
1 tablespoon oil (for dough)
$7^1/_2$ ounces warm water (for kneading)
Filling:
5 medium potatoes, boiled and mashed
1 teaspoon salt
$^1/_2$ teaspoon red chili powder
$1^1/_2$ teaspoons dry mango powder (amchur)
$^1/_2$ teaspoon garam masala
2 green chilies, finely chopped
1 teaspoon ginger, grated
2 tablespoons coriander, finely chopped

$^1/_2$ cup whole wheat flour (for rolling)
$^1/_2$ cup oil (for cooking)
Butter as needed (optional)

Method:

Mix flour, salt and oil. Add a little water at a time and knead dough until it no longer sticks to the bowl.
❦ *TLC Tip: It may help to put some oil on your hands to prevent dough from sticking to fingers.*
Sprinkle a few drops of water, cover and set aside for $^1/_2$ hour.

For filling, mix all ingredients and divide into 10 equal portions.

Knead dough again, and make 10 equal balls. Coat balls with flour. (This prevents them from sticking to the rolling board). Lightly press balls to about 3 inch diameter between the palms. Spread a little oil on one side and add one portion of the filling in the center. Fold edges from all sides to cover the filling. Flatten between palms again. Apply flour to both sides. Using pin, roll into 5-6 inches in diameter using moderate and uniform pressure. (Apply flour as necessary to prevent sticking).

Heat tawa for 2 to 3 minutes over medium heat. Apply a little oil uniformly on it (*this step does not have to be repeated for subsequent paranthas*). Place parantha on tawa and wait until small bubbles appear on surface. Turn it over with a pair of tongs and apply a little oil to top surface. Turn it over again. Apply a little oil and this time press lightly with back of cooking spoon to help it puff up. Wait until surface turns golden brown. Turn it over once more and let other side turn golden brown. Remove and serve or stack for serving later.

❦ *TLC Tip: For parantha to puff up; center has to be of same thickness or slightly thicker than edges when rolling. This comes with practice. Don't lose heart if first few paranthas do not puff up.*

❦ *TLC Tip: In the beginning it may be advisable to remove tawa from burner to prevent overheating while next parantha is being rolled. However, make sure it is heated again for next parantha.*

For help: www.momsindiancooking.com

Serving suggestion
Serve hot with yogurt, achar or sukhi matar. Optionally, a little butter can be applied to hot parantha before eating.

Preferred kitchenware:
- *2 qt. mixing bowl*
- *Flour board*
- *Rolling pin*
- *Tawa or medium size nonstick frying pan*
- *Cooking spoon*
- *Tongs*

Gobhi Parantha

North Indian Shallow Fried Bread Filled with Cauliflower

Makes about 10

Preparation time: 1 hr.
Cooking time: 5 mins. each

Ingredients:

2 cups whole wheat flour for dough
$^1/_2$ teaspoon salt
1 tablespoon oil (for dough)
$7^1/_2$ ounces warm water (for kneading)
Filling:
2 cups cauliflower, finely grated (press between layers of paper towel or cheese cloth to remove excess moisture)
1 teaspoon salt
$^1/_2$ teaspoon red chili powder
$1^1/_2$ teaspoons dry mango powder (amchur)
$^1/_2$ teaspoon garam masala
2 green chilies, finely chopped
1 teaspoon ginger, grated
2 tablespoons coriander, finely chopped

$^1/_2$ cup whole wheat flour (for rolling)
$^1/_2$ cup oil (for cooking)
Butter as needed (optional)

Method:

Mix flour, salt and oil. Add a little water at a time and knead dough until it no longer sticks to the bowl.
☙ *TLC Tip: It may help to put some oil on your hands to prevent dough from sticking to fingers.*
Sprinkle a few drops of water, cover and set aside for $^1/_2$ hour.

For filling, mix all ingredients and divide into 10 equal portions.

Knead dough again, and make 10 equal balls. Coat balls with flour. (This prevents them from sticking to the rolling board). Lightly press balls to about 3 inch diameter between the palms. Spread a little oil on one side and add one portion of the filling in the center. Fold edges from all sides to cover the filling. Flatten between palms again. Apply flour to both sides. Using pin roll into 5-6 inches in diameter using moderate and uniform pressure. (Apply flour as necessary to prevent sticking).

Heat tawa for 2 to 3 minutes over medium heat. Apply a little oil uniformly on it (*this step does not have to be repeated for subsequent paranthas*). Place parantha on tawa and wait until small bubbles appear on surface. Turn it over with a pair of tongs and apply a little oil to top surface. Turn it over again. Apply a little oil and this time press lightly with back of cooking spoon to help it puff up. Wait until surface turns golden brown. Turn it over once more and let other side turn golden brown. Remove and serve or stack for serving later.

❦ *TLC Tip: For parantha to puff up, center has to be of same thickness or slightly thicker than edges when rolling. This comes with practice. Don't lose heart if first few paranthas do not puff up.*

❦ *TLC Tip: In the beginning it may be advisable to remove tawa from burner to prevent overheating while next parantha is being rolled. However, make sure it is heated again for next parantha.*

Serving suggestion
Serve hot with yogurt, achar or pineapple subzi. Optionally, a little butter can be applied to hot parantha before eating.

Preferred kitchenware
- *2 qt. mixing bowl*
- *Flour board*
- *Rolling pin*
- *Tawa/medium size non stick pan*
- *Cooking spoon*
- *Tongs*

For help: www.momsindiancooking.com

Matar Parantha

North Indian Shallow Fried Bread
Filled with Peas

Makes about 10

Preparation time: 1 hr.
Cooking time: 5 mins. each

Ingredients:

2 cups whole wheat flour (for dough)
$^1/_2$ teaspoon salt
1 tablespoon oil (for dough)
$7^1/_2$ ounces warm water (for kneading)
Filling:
2 cups peas, boiled and mashed
1 teaspoon salt
$^1/_2$ teaspoon red chili powder
$1^1/_2$ teaspoons dry mango powder (amchur)
$^1/_2$ teaspoon garam masala
2 green chilies, finely chopped
1 teaspoon ginger, grated
2 tablespoons coriander, finely chopped

$^1/_2$ cup whole wheat flour (for rolling)
$^1/_2$ cup oil (for cooking)
Butter as needed (optional)

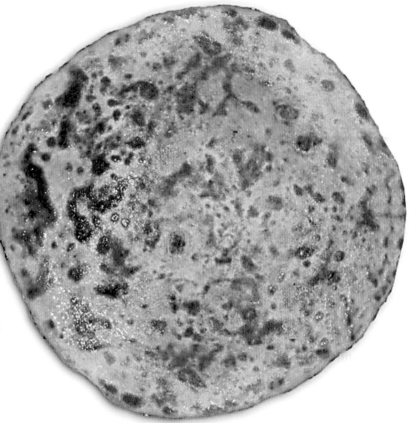

Method:

Mix flour, salt and oil. Add a little water at a time and knead dough until it no longer sticks to the bowl.
☙ *TLC Tip: It may help to put some oil on your hands to prevent dough from sticking to fingers.*
Sprinkle a few drops of water, cover and set aside for $^1/_2$ hour.
For filling, mix all ingredients and divide into 10 equal portions.
Knead dough again and make 10 equal balls. Coat balls with dry flour. (This prevents them from sticking to the rolling board). Lightly press balls to about 3 inch diameter between the palms. Spread a little oil on one side and add one portion of

the filling in the center. Fold edges from all sides to cover the filling. Flatten between palms again. Apply flour to both sides. Using pin, roll into 5-6 inches in diameter using moderate and uniform pressure. (Apply flour as necessary to prevent sticking).

Heat tawa for 2 to 3 minutes over medium heat. Apply a little oil uniformly on it (*this step does not have to be repeated for subsequent paranthas*). Place parantha on tawa and wait until small bubbles appear on surface. Turn it over with a pair of tongs and apply a little oil to top surface. Turn it over again. Apply a little oil and this time press lightly with back of cooking spoon to help it puff up. Wait until surface turns golden brown. Turn it over once more and let other side turn golden brown. Remove and serve or stack for serving later.

❦ *TLC Tip: For parantha to puff up, center has to be of same thickness or slightly thicker than edges when rolling. This comes with practice. Don't lose heart if first few paranthas do not puff up.*

❦ *TLC Tip: In the beginning it may be advisable to remove tawa from burner to prevent overheating while next parantha is being rolled. However, make sure it is heated again for next parantha.*

For help: www.momsindiancooking.com

Serving suggestion
Serve hot with yogurt, achar or pineapple subzi. Optionally, a little butter can be applied to the hot parantha before eating.

Preferred kitchenware
- *2 qt. mixing bowl*
- *Flour board*
- *Rolling pin*
- *Tawa/medium sized non stick pan*
- *Cooking spoon*
- *Tongs*

Paneer Parantha

North Indian Shallow Fried Bread Filled with Cheese

Makes about 10

Preparation time: 1 hr.
Cooking time: 5 mins. each

Ingredients:

2 cups whole wheat flour (for dough)
$1/_2$ teaspoon salt
1 tablespoon oil (for dough)
$71/_2$ ounces warm water (for kneading)
Filling:
1 cup paneer, mashed
See recipe on page 171
1 teaspoon salt
$1/_2$ teaspoon red chili powder
$11/_2$ teaspoons dry mango powder (amchur)
$1/_2$ teaspoon garam masala
2 green chilies, finely chopped
1 teaspoon ginger, grated
2 tablespoons coriander, finely chopped

$1/_2$ cup whole wheat flour (for rolling)
$1/_2$ cup oil (for cooking)
Butter as needed (optional)

Method:

Mix flour, salt and oil. Add a little water at a time and knead dough until it no longer sticks to bowl.
❦TLC Tip: It may help to put some oil on your hands to prevent dough from sticking to fingers.
Sprinkle a few drops of water, cover and set aside for $1/_2$ hour.
For filling, mix all ingredients and divide into 10 equal portions.
Knead dough again and make 10 equal balls. Coat balls with dry flour. (This prevents them from sticking to the rolling board). Lightly press balls into about 3 inch diameter between the palms. Spread a little oil on one side and add one portion of

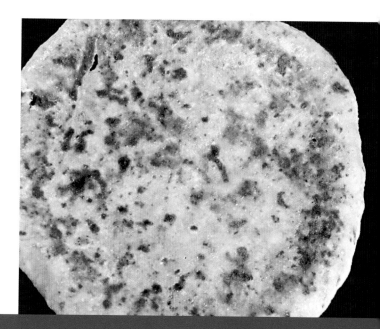

101

the filling in the center. Fold edges from all sides to cover the filling. Flatten between palms again. Apply flour to both sides. Using pin, roll into 5-6 inches in diameter using moderate and uniform pressure. (Apply flour as necessary to prevent sticking).

Heat tawa for 2 to 3 minutes over medium heat. Apply a little oil uniformly on it (*this step does not have to be repeated for subsequent paranthas*). Place parantha on tawa and wait until small bubbles appear on surface. Turn it over with a pair of tongs and apply a little oil to top surface. Turn it over again. Apply a little oil and this time press lightly with back of cooking spoon to help it puff up. Wait until surface turns golden brown. Turn it over once more and let other side turn golden brown. Remove and serve or stack for serving later.

🐾 *TLC Tip: For parantha to puff up, center has to be of same thickness or slightly thicker than edges when rolling. This comes with practice. Don't lose heart if first few paranthas do not puff up.*

🐾 *TLC Tip: In the beginning it may be advisable to remove tawa from burner to prevent overheating while next parantha is being rolled. However, make sure it is heated again for next parantha.*

For help: www.momsindiancooking.com

Serving suggestion
Serve hot with yogurt, achar or pineapple subzi. Optionally, a little butter can be applied to the hot parantha before eating.

Preferred kitchenware
- *2 qt. mixing bowl*
- *Flour board*
- *Rolling pin*
- *Tawa /medium size non stick pan*
- *Cooking spoon*
- *Tongs*

Sada Parantha
North Indian Shallow Fried Bread
Makes about 10

Preparation time: 45 mins.
Cooking time: 3 mins. each

Ingredients:

2 cups whole wheat flour (dough)
$1/_2$ teaspoon salt
1 tablespoon oil (for dough)
$7^1/_2$ ounces warm water (for kneading)
$1/_2$ cup whole wheat flour (for rolling)
$1/_2$ cup oil (for cooking)

Method:

Mix flour, salt and oil. Add a little water at a time and knead dough until it no longer sticks to the bowl.

🍵 *TLC Tip: It may help to put some oil on your hands to prevent dough from sticking to fingers.*

Sprinkle a few drops of water, cover and set aside for $1/_2$ hour.

Knead dough again and make 10 equal balls. Coat balls with flour. (This prevents them from sticking to the rolling board). Lightly press balls to about 3 inch diameter between the palms. Spread a little oil on one side. Fold edges from all sides. Flatten between palms again. Apply dry flour to both sides. Using pin, roll into 5-6 inches in diameter using moderate and uniform pressure. (Apply flour as necessary to prevent sticking).

Heat tawa for 2 to 3 minutes over medium heat. Apply a little oil uniformly on it (*this step does not have to be repeated for subsequent paranthas*). Place parantha on tawa and wait until small bubbles appear on surface. Turn it over with a pair of tongs and apply a little oil to top surface. Turn it over again. Apply a little oil and this time press lightly with back of cooking spoon to help it puff up. Wait until surface turns golden brown. Turn it over once more and let other side turn golden brown. Remove and serve or stack for serving later.

🍵 *TLC Tip: For parantha to puff up, center has to be of same thickness or slightly thicker than edges when rolling. This comes with practice. Don't lose heart if first few paranthas do not puff up.*

🍵 *TLC Tip: In the beginning it may be advisable to remove tawa from burner to prevent overheating while next parantha is being rolled. However, make sure it is heated again for next parantha.*

For help: www.momsindiancooking.com

Serving suggestion
Serve hot with bhindi, raita and dahi ke alu or other vegetable or meat curries.

Preferred kitchenware
• *2 qt. mixing bowl*
• *Flour board*
• *Rolling pin*
• *Tawa/medium size nonstick pan*
• *Cooking spoon*
• *Tongs*

Poori
Deep Fried Bread
Makes about 16

Preparation time: 30 mins.
Cooking time: 2 mins. each

Ingredients:
2 cups whole wheat flour
$^1/_2$ teaspoon salt
1 tablespoon oil (for kneading)
5-6 ounces warm water (for kneading)
2-3 tablespoons oil (for rolling)
2-3 cups oil (for frying)

Method:
Mix flour, salt and oil in bowl. Add water and knead dough until it does not stick to bowl any more.

☙ *TLC Tip: It may help to put some oil on your hands to prevent dough from sticking to fingers.*
Cover and set aside for 15 minutes.
Knead and divide dough into 16 equal parts. Take each portion, one at a time and squeeze between hands and shape into a ball. Lightly press each ball between hands to flatten to about 2 inch diameter. Lightly apply oil to rolling pin and flour board. Roll out with rolling pin to approximately 4 inch diameter.

☙ *TLC Tip: While rolling, apply a little oil to dough 2 to 3 times to prevent sticking to flour board.*
Heat oil in kadhai over medium-high heat.

☙ *TLC Tip: To test if oil is hot enough, take a pinch of dough and put into oil. If it rises to surface quickly, oil is ready. When oil is hot, add 1 poori at a time.*

☙ *TLC Tip: Slide poori in from side of kadhai. Do not drop in middle. Splashed oil can cause serious burns.*
It may help the puffing if you keep pressing poori in oil with a very light pressure with slotted spoon. When one side has turned light brown, fry the other side. Drain excess oil and remove. Serve hot or stack and reheat in oven before serving

❗Caution: Never leave oil unattended over a stove. If overheated, the oil can catch fire, causing serious injury

Serving suggestion
Serve with sukhe alu, amras or other vegetable of choice.
To serve later, wrap in aluminum foil and heat in a warm oven for a few minutes.

Preferred kitchenware
- *2 qt. mixing bowl*
- *Flour board*
- *Rolling pin*
- *Kadhai or deep frying pan*
- *Jharar (slotted spoon)*

For help: www.momsindiancooking.com

Roti *aka* **Phulka** *aka* **Chapati**

Roasted Flat Whole Wheat Bread

Makes about 10

Preparation time: 45 mins.
Cooking time: 2 mins. each

Ingredients:

7¹/₂ ounces warm water
2 cups whole wheat flour (for dough)
¹/₄ cup whole wheat flour (for rolling)
Butter (optional)

Method:

Add a little water at a time to flour and knead dough until it no longer sticks to bowl. ❧*TLC Tip: It may help to put some oil on your hands to prevent dough from sticking to fingers.* Sprinkle a few drops of water, cover and set aside for about ¹/₂ hour.

Knead dough again, and make 10 equal balls. Apply flour on all sides of ball to prevent sticking to flour board. Lightly press balls between hands and flatten to about 2 inch diameter.

Flatten dough out with rolling pin, using moderate and uniform pressure, to about 5 to 6 inch diameter. ❧ *TLC Tip: You may need to apply dry flour once again to prevent from sticking to board.*

Heat tawa for about 2 to 3 minutes over medium heat. Turn on additional burner on medium heat. If electric, place cake rack over burner. Place roti on tawa. Wait until very small bubbles appear on top then flip over. Cook other side until brown spots appear. Using tongs, pick roti up from tawa and put it on other burner, flipping it over in the process. When it has puffed and turned golden brown, turn it over and cook the other side.❧*TLC Tip: It helps to press lightly with tongs to make roti puff up uniformly.*

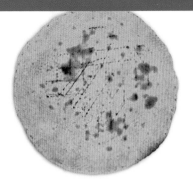

Remove from burner and apply butter to one side (optional).

❧*TLC Tip: In order to have roti puff up properly, the center has to be same or slightly thicker than the edges when rolling. This comes with experience. Do not lose heart if the first few rotis do not puff up.*

❧*TLC Tip: For beginnners, it may be advisable to remove tawa from burner to prevent it from overheating while roti is cooking on open burner. If you do remove tawa from burner, make sure it is hot again when you are ready for next roti.*

❧*TLC Tip: To cook extra rotis for futher use, cook rotis on tawa and skip the stage of cooking directly on burner. Freeze these and just before serving, puff them up in a toaster oven on toast setting. They puff just as though they were freshly done.*

Serving suggestion
Roti is a basic bread that can be served with any Indian food. In Indian homes, it is often served with dal, vegetable and raita.

Preferred kitchenware
• *2 qt. mixing bowl*
• *Flour board*
• *Rolling pin*
• *Tawa or medium round non stick pan*
• *Tongs*
• *Cake-cooling rack (small grill to place over electric element; not needed for gas burners-refer to photo on page 9).*

For help: www.momsindiancooking.com

Tandoori* Roti

Oven Roasted Flat Whole Wheat Bread

Makes about 10

Preparation time: 2 hrs. 15 mins.
Cooking time: 20 mins.

Ingredients:

2 cups whole wheat flour (for dough)
$^1/_4$ teaspoon salt
2 tablespoons oil
$^1/_8$ teaspoon baking soda
$2^1/_2$ tablespoons plain yogurt
$^1/_2$ cup warm water (for kneading)
$^1/_4$ cup whole wheat flour (for rolling)
Butter as needed (optional)

Method:

Mix well 2 cups of flour, salt, oil and baking soda in bowl. Add yogurt and water. Knead dough until it no longer sticks to bowl.
TLC Tip: It may help to put some oil on your hands to prevent dough from sticking to fingers.
Cover and set aside for about 2 hours.
Knead dough again and divide into 10 equal balls. Lightly press between your hands and flatten to about 2 inch diameter. Apply flour on both sides to prevent sticking to flour board. Flatten dough with rolling pin using moderate and uniform pressure to about 4-5 inches diameter. Apply flour once again to prevent from sticking to board.
Preheat oven on broil setting. Spread aluminum foil on top rack and place 3-4 rotis at a time on it. When rotis have puffed and turned golden brown, flip and bake other side. Remove and apply butter to one side (optional). Serve hot.

* Tandoor is a circular open clay oven with burning charcoal at the bottom. Tandoori rotis are traditionally baked by sticking them on the interior wall of the tandoor.

Serving suggestions
Tandoori rotis go well with meat and chicken dishes. They can also be served with Rajma (kidney beans) or Chhole

Preferred kitchenware
- *2 qt. mixing bowl*
- *Flour board*
- *Rolling pin*
- *Aluminum foil*

For help: www.momsindiancooking.com

Rice Dishes

Brown Basmati Rice

A healthier alternative to white rice. Grown in the foothills of the Himalayas, its aromatic and nut-like taste makes this rice a tasty complement to most dishes.

Serves 4

Preparation time: 5 mins.
Cooking time: 20 mins.

Ingredients:

1 cup brown basmati rice
2 cups water
$^1/_2$ teaspoon salt (optional)
2 tablespoons ghee or butter

Method:

Rinse rice thoroughly 2 to 3 times. Drain. For softer rice, use 1 cup of rice to 2 cups of water; for firmer rice, use 1 cup of rice to $1^1/_4$ cups of water. Combine rice and water (add salt if desired) in a heavy saucepan. Bring to a boil. Cover, turn heat down, and let simmer for 10-15 minutes, or until all water is absorbed. Fluff with a fork. Add ghee or butter before serving.

Serving suggestion
Eat with any of dals or variants.

Preferred kitchenware
• *2qt. saucepan with lid*

Dahi Bhat
South Indian Style Rice with Yogurt
Serves 4

Preparation time: 1 hr.
Cooking time: 25 mins.

Ingredients:

2 cups plain, cooked basmati rice
See recipe on page 110
3 cups of plain yogurt
$1^1/_2$ teaspoons salt
1 teaspoon green chili, chopped
2 tablespoons coriander, chopped
For tempering:
$1^1/_2$ tablespoons oil
$1^1/_2$ teaspoons urad dal
1 teaspoon mustard seeds
1 dried whole red chili
5-6 curry leaves

Method:

Make sure rice is at room temperature. It may be better to prepare the dish an hour before serving for ingredients to mix completely.
Mix all ingredients together (*other than those for tempering*).
Heat oil in frying pan over medium heat.
Add dal. Fry until golden brown. Add mustard seeds. When mustard seeds start to pop, add whole red chili and curry leaves. Remove from heat and mix with rice mixture. This dish is normally eaten at room temperature.

Serving suggestion
Serve as a side dish with any meal or a healthy snack by itself.

Preferred kitchenware
• *2 qt. mixing bowl*
• *Very small frying pan*

Khichdi
Rice with Mung Dal

Khichdi is an easily digestable, flavorful meal that provides a change from heavy-to-digest food.

Serves 4

Preparation time: 35 mins.
Cooking time: 25 mins.

Ingredients:

1 cup washed, split mung dal
1 cup long grain rice
2 tablespoons oil
4 cloves
Pinch of asafetida
$1^1/_4$ teaspoons salt
$6^1/_2$ cups water
$^1/_2$ teaspoon turmeric powder
$^1/_2$ teaspoon garam masala
2 tablespoons ghee

Method:

Mix dal and rice in bowl and wash 3 to 4 times. Soak for 30 minutes. Drain. Heat oil in pressure cooker on medium heat. Add cloves, asafetida, dal, rice, salt, water and turmeric powder. Stir, close lid and turn heat on high. When steam starts to come out, put the weight on. Turn heat back to medium and wait for whistle. Reduce heat to low. Cook for 5 minutes, remove from heat and set aside for 15 minutes. Make sure all steam has dissipated before opening lid. Add garam masala and ghee. Stir and serve.

❦TLC Tip: *If you like your Khichdi a little thinner you can add a little boiling water and mix.*

Serving suggestion
Serve with plain yogurt, achar and roasted papad. Optionally, add about 1 teaspoon of ghee to each serving.

Preferred kitchenware
• *4 qt. pressure cooker*
• *2 qt. mixing bowl*

Plain or Cumin Basmati Rice

Grown in the foothills of the Himalayas, this aromatic rice is a tasty complement to most dishes.

Serves 4

Preparation time: 35 mins.
Cooking time: 20 mins.

Ingredients:

1 cup basmati rice
2 cups water
2 tablespoons ghee or butter
1 teaspoon cumin seeds*
$^{1}/_{2}$ teaspoon salt*

Method:

Wash rice 3-4 times and soak for 30 minutes. Drain. Add 2 cups of water to rice. Bring mixture to boil on medium-high heat. Reduce heat to low, cover and simmer 10-12 minutes until rice becomes soft. Remove from heat, set aside for 5 minutes. Add ghee or butter and serve hot.

* *For Cumin Rice*: Heat ghee in saucepan on medium heat. Add cumin seeds. When cumin seeds start to pop, add rice, water and salt. On medium-high heat bring mixture to boil. Reduce heat to low, cover and simmer 10-12 minutes until rice becomes soft. Remove from heat, set aside for 5 minutes. Serve hot.

Serving suggestion
Serve with dal, vegetables or any meat dishes.

Preferred kitchenware
2 qt. saucepan with lid

Chicken Biryani
Spicy Fried Rice with Chicken
Serves 4

Preparation time: 30 mins.
Cooking time: 70 mins.

Ingredients:

2 cups basmati Rice
12 cups water
$1/2$ teaspoon turmeric powder
4 tablespoons oil
6 cloves
1 small piece cinnamon
4 black cardamoms
8 peppercorns
4 bay leaves
1 large onion, sliced
1 teaspoon garlic, chopped
1 tablespoon ginger, chopped
$1/2$ teaspoon salt
2 tablespoons biryani masala*
1 cup tomatoes, crushed
8 chicken thighs
$1/2$ cup water
$1/2$ teaspoon garam masala
For garnish:
1 large red onion, thinly sliced
2 medium tomatoes, sliced

*Available in Indian grocery stores

Method:

Wash and soak rice for 10 minutes. Put 6 cups of water and 1 cup of rice in small saucepan over high heat. Bring to a boil. Turn heat to medium and cook until rice is cooked to a point where there is a slight hard core left.

🍒 *TLC Tip: This can be checked by taking out a grain of rice, pressing against a spoon and feeling the slightly hard core.* Strain and keep aside in bowl.

Repeat the same with the other cup of rice except in this case, add turmeric powder to water and rice mixture. Heat oil in large saucepan over medium heat. Add cloves, cinnamon, black cardamoms, peppercorns and bay leaves. When leaves turn brown, add onions, garlic and ginger. Sauté until onions turn golden brown. Add salt and biryani masala. Cook for 2 minutes and add tomatoes. Cook for another 5 to 7 minutes on medium-low heat. Add chicken and $1/2$ cup water. Cook until chicken becomes soft.

Preheat oven to 350 degrees F. In glass tray, put layers (in the order written) of white rice, half the chicken, yellow rice and the other half of chicken. Cover with foil. Bake in oven for 30 minutes.

Sprinkle with garam masala and garnish with onions and tomatoes.

Serving suggestions
As a main meal with raita or as a side dish for a party.

Preferred kitchenware
- *Large glass serving dish (that can be heated to about 350 deg F)*
- *2 qt. sauce pan*
- *4 qt. sauce pan*
- *Aluminum foil*
- *Large strainer*
- *Medium bowl*

Tahari *aka* **Pulao**
Delicately Spiced Rice with Vegetables
Serves 4

Preparation time: 30 mins.
Cooking time: 30 mins.

Ingredients:

1 cup basmati rice
4 tablespoons oil
$1/4$ teaspoon cumin seeds
4 bay leaves
1 two inch piece of cinnamon stick
2 black cardamoms
$1/4$ cup cashew nuts
$1/2$ teaspoon mustard seeds
4 cloves
1 medium onion, sliced
$1/4$ teaspoon turmeric powder
1 teaspoon salt
$1/4$ teaspoon red chili powder
$1/2$ teaspoon garam masala
$1/4$ cup raisins (optional)
1 cup cauliflower, cut into about one inch pieces
$1/2$ cup peas, fresh or thawed
1 medium potato, cut into one inch cubes
$2^1/2$ cups water
1 tablespoon coriander, chopped

Method:

Wash rice 3-4 times and soak for 10 minutes. Heat oil in pan on medium-high heat. Add cumin seeds, bay leaves, cinnamon, black cardamoms, cashew nuts, mustard seeds and cloves. When seeds start to pop, add onions and cook until light brown. Add turmeric powder, salt, red chili powder, garam masala, rice, raisins, vegetables and keep stirring for 2 minutes. Add water, bring to a boil and reduce heat to low. Cover and let cook for about 15 minutes, stirring gently once or twice. Turn off heat and leave on stove for 10 minutes. Before serving, garnish with chopped coriander.

Serving suggestion
Serve with plain yogurt, achar and roasted papad.

Preferred kitchenware
• *4 qt. saucepan with lid*

Non Vegetarian Dishes

Chicken Curry

Serves 4

Preparation time: 15 mins.
Cooking time: 35 mins.

Ingredients:

2 lb chicken thighs or drumsticks
1 cup precooked masala
See recipe on page 172
1 teaspoon salt
10 pieces raw cashew nuts, ground
2 cups water
1 teaspoon garam masala*
2 tablespoons coriander, chopped
* Available from Indian stores or see recipe
page 174

Method:

Remove skin from chicken.

Heat saucepan on medium high heat. Add
precooked masala, salt and ground cashew. Stir.
Add water and chicken pieces. When the mixture
starts to boil, cover and turn heat to medium low.
Cook for about 30 minutes or until chicken gets
soft, stirring occasionally. Add garam masala,
stir and turn heat off.

Garnish with chopped coriander.

Serving suggestion
*Serve with nans or rotis with a side
of onion slices marinated in salt
and lemon juice.*

Preferred kitchenware
• *4 qt. sauce pan with lid*
• *Coffee grinder*

Chicken Makhani
Butter Chicken
Serves 4

Preparation time: 2 hrs. 15 mins.
Cooking time: 45 mins.

Ingredients:
For marinating:
1 cup plain yogurt
$1/_2$ teaspoon ginger paste
$1/_2$ teaspoon garlic paste
4 tablespoons tandoori chicken masala*
2 tablespoons lemon juice
2 lb skinned boneless chicken thighs/breasts
cut into $1^1/_2$ inch pieces
For sauce:
2 tablespoons cashew nuts (soaked
in 4 tablespoons of milk)
$1/_4$ cup oil for basting
2 tablespoons butter
$1/_2$ teaspoon ginger paste
$1/_2$ teaspoon garlic paste
1 medium green chili, slit
2 cups tomato puree
$1/_2$ teaspoon salt
1 pint half and half or whole milk
1 teaspoon garam masala
2 tablespoons coriander, chopped

*Available in Indian grocery stores

Method:
Whisk yogurt with ginger, garlic, tandoori masala and lemon juice. Add chicken, cover and marinate for 2 hours at room temperature. Grind cashew nuts and milk to a fine paste.

Preheat oven to broil setting. Broil chicken until evenly golden brown, occasionally basting with oil and turning. (Save the left over marinade for later use).

Heat butter in saucepan over medium heat. Add ginger, garlic paste and slit green chili. Sauté for 2 minutes, add tomato puree, left over marinade, salt and cashew paste. Mix and let simmer for 5 to 7 minutes on medium-low heat. Add chicken and cook for 10 minutes on low heat. Add half and half or milk and garam masala. Simmer for 2 to 3 minutes. Garnish with chopped coriander.

Serving suggestion
Serve with nans or rotis with a side of onion slices marinated in salt and lemon juice.

Preferred kitchenware
- *4 qt. sauce pan*
- *Broiling tray*
- *4 qt. mixing bowl with lid*
- *Blender*

Chicken Malai Kabab for BBQ

Serves 4

Preparation time: 2 hrs. 15 mins. (overnight preferred)
Cooking time: 20 mins.

Ingredients:

$^1/_2$ teaspoon garam masala
$^1/_4$ cup precooked masala
See recipe page 172
$^1/_4$ cup plain yogurt
$^1/_2$ pint cream
2 tablespoons lemon juice
$^1/_2$ teaspoon salt
1 lb boneless chicken strips
$^1/_4$ cup ghee or butter

Method:

Mix garam masala, precooked masala, yogurt, cream, lemon juice and salt together in large bowl and marinate the strips of chicken in mixture for at least 2 hours. *

Weave marinated chicken strips onto skewers (like satay) and place on grill, basting with ghee until completely grilled.

*Taste is much fuller if you can marinate chicken overnight in refrigerator.

☙ *TLC Tip: To prevent wooden skewers from burning, be sure to soak them in water for several hours before using.*

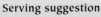

Serving suggestion
This dish goes well with any type of chutney and onions in lemon.

Preferred kitchenware
- *Skewers*
- *Barbeque grill*
- *2 qt. mixing bowl*

Chicken or Lamb Seekh Kabab
Serves 4

Preparation time: 8 hrs. 30 mins.
Cooking time: 20 mins.

Ingredients:
2 medium green chilies
1$^1/_2$ teaspoons ginger
1 teaspoon garlic
$^1/_2$ meduim onion
4 tablespoons gram flour (besan)
1 lb ground chicken or lamb
1 teaspoon salt
2 pieces black cardamom, ground
1 teaspoon garam masala
6 tablespoons bread crumbs
2 tablespoons yogurt
2 teaspoons lemon juice
$^1/_2$ egg, beaten
Oil for basting
To garnish:
2 tablespoons chat masala*
1 teaspoon garam masala
2 tablespoons coriander, chopped
1 medium onion, sliced
1 lemon cut in fourths, lengthwise

*Available in Indian grocery stores

Method:
Grind green chilies, ginger, garlic and onion in food processor to a coarse paste.

Heat frying pan over medium-low heat and roast gram flour until light brown. Let cool.

Mix well gram flour and all ingredients except egg and oil in bowl. Cover and marinate for 8 hours in refrigerator or 4 hours at room temperature.

Preheat oven to 400 degrees F. Add beaten egg to meat, mix and shape into 1 inch diameter by 6-7 inch long rolls over the middle of dowels. Arrange in tray so that the dowel ends overhang the opposite edges about 1 inch. Brush lightly with oil, and place in the middle rack for 15 minutes. Turn oven to broil setting. Place dowels so that one end rests over one edge of tray and one end is inside tray. This facilitates

Suggested arrangement of Kababs before baking

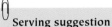

Serving suggestion
This dish goes well with any type of chutney and onions in lemon and can be used as hors d'oeuvre before dinner or any time snack.

Preferred kitchenware
- *Food processor*
- *2 qt. mixing bowl*
- *Small frying pan*
- *7x8 inch disposable aluminum tray*
- *3/8 inch round wooden dowels cut nine inches long*
- *Brush for basting*

Optional :
- *Baking tray*
- *Foil to cover baking tray*

the turning of the dowels. Broil for 6-8 minutes, turning dowels every minute or so to brown kababs evenly all around. Baste as necessary while broiling. Gently twist kababs on dowel to separate and carefully push out. Before serving, sprinkle with chat and garam masala and garnish with coriander, onion and lemon.

Alternately, make about 3 by 4 inch oval patties about 1/2 inch think. Place a piece of foil on a baking tray, grease and put the patties in the middle rack and bake as above. For broiling, turn the patties over one time for even broiling on both sides. Can also be barbecued. How about a mouth waterning Kabab burger?

🍃 *TLC Tip: Wooden dowels are available in hardware stores in lengths of 48 inches for about a dollar each. Cut them into lengths of 9 inches each. If you do not have a saw, use a bread knife to score the dowel all round and break along the score.*

Kadhai Chicken

Serves 4

Preparation time: 40 mins.
Cooking time: 30 mins.

Ingredients:

1 teaspoon coriander seeds
4 whole red chilies
6 tablespoons oil
4 cloves
2 black cardamoms
1 two inch piece of cinnamon stick
2 tablespoons ginger paste
2 tablespoons garlic paste
2 medium onions, sliced
4 small green chilies, chopped
2 teaspoons coriander powder
1 teaspoon chili powder
$^1/_2$ teaspoon turmeric powder
1 teaspoon salt
3 large tomatoes, chopped
2 lbs skinless, boneless chicken thighs cut into $1^1/_2$ inch pieces
1 green bell pepper, cut into 1 inch squares
1 red bell pepper, cut into 1 inch squares
$^3/_4$ teaspoon garam masala
1 teaspoon paprika
2 tablespoons coriander, chopped

Serving suggestion
Serve with rotis, nans, or paranthas with onions in lemon.

Preferred kitchenware
• *Medium kadhai or deep frying pan*
• *Mortar and pestle*

Method:

Crush coriander seeds and whole red chilies together in mortar and keep aside.

Heat oil in kadhai or deep frying pan on medium high heat. Add cloves, cardamoms, cinnamon stick, crushed coriander seeds and chilies, ginger and garlic pastes. Sauté for 1 minute. Add onion and green chilies and sauté until onions are golden brown. Add coriander powder, red chili powder, turmeric powder and salt. Keep stirring for 1 more minute. Add tomatoes and turn heat to medium. Stir for 5-7 minutes or until oil separates. Add chicken pieces, stir, cover and turn heat to medium-low. Cook for about 8-10 minutes stirring a few times. Add bell peppers, garam masala and paprika and cook uncovered for another 4 minutes. Add chopped coriander before serving.

Palak (Spinach) Chicken

Serves 4

Preparation time: 1 hr.
Cooking time: 45 mins.

Ingredients:

$1^1/_2$ cups chopped spinach, thawed
$1^1/_4$ cups water
2 tablespoons oil (for spinach)
Whole garam masala:
1 half inch piece of cinnamon stick
6 cloves
2 black cardamoms
4 green cardamoms
2 bay leaves
8 peppercorns

1 medium onion, chopped finely
1 tablespoon garlic, chopped
1 teaspoon ginger, chopped
1 tablespoon green chili, chopped
1 teaspoon salt
$^1/_2$ teaspoon turmeric powder
4 tablespoons coriander powder
$^1/_2$ teaspoon red chili powder
1 cup tomato puree
6 tablespoons oil (for chicken)
8 chicken thighs, skinless
$^1/_2$ teaspoon garam masala

Serving suggestion
Serve with rotis or paranthas with a side vegetable and onions in lemon.

Preferred kitchenware
- *2 Medium kadhai or deep frying pans*
- *Blender*

Method:

Grind spinach with water and keep aside.
Heat oil in kadhai or frying pan on medium heat. Add whole garam masala ingredients and stir until brown. Add onions, garlic, ginger and green chilies. Sauté for 4 to 5 minutes until onion mixture is golden brown. Add salt, turmeric powder, coriander powder and red chili powder. Stir and add tomato puree. Turn heat to medium-low, cook for 5 to 7 minutes. Add spinach. Turn heat off and let stand.
Heat 6 tablespoons of oil in kadhai or frying pan on high heat. Add chicken. Keep turning and stirring until it gets white on all sides. Add spinach mixture, stir and simmer on low heat for 30 minutes until chicken is soft. Add garam masala.

Rajasthani Chicken
Colorful Spicy Chicken from Rajasthan
Serves 4

Preparation time: 6 hrs.
Cooking time: 30 mins.

Ingredients:
8 pieces chicken thighs, skinned
Marinating - Step 1:
2 tablespoons lemon juice
$^1/_2$ teaspoon red chili powder
$^1/_2$ teaspoon salt
Marinating - Step 2:
3 tablespoons oil (to sauté)
1 large onion, chopped
4 cloves of garlic, peeled and chopped
$^1/_2$ cup almonds, blanched
1 one-inch piece of ginger, peeled and chopped
1 teaspoon red chili powder
$^1/_2$ teaspoon salt
8 oz plain yogurt
$^1/_4$ teaspoon red food color
$^1/_4$ teaspoon yellow food color
4 oz melted ghee or butter
To garnish:
1 large onion, sliced
1 lemon, cut into wedges
4-5 sprigs of coriander leaves

Method:
Marinate - Step 1: Wash chicken pieces and dry with paper towel. Slit the pieces deeply and marinate with lemon juice, red chili powder and salt. Set aside for 1 hour.
Marinate -Step 2: Heat oil in frying pan on medium heat. Sauté onions until light brown. Add chopped garlic and continue to sauté. Add almonds. Stir and turn off the stove. Let cool. Pour

mixture into blender. Add ginger, chili powder, salt and yogurt. Blend into fine paste. Put in bowl, add colors and mix well. Put the pieces of chicken in this mixture and rub in the marinade into slits. Mix and set aside for 4 hours or overnight in refrigerator.

Thaw chicken, if refrigerated. Preheat oven to 400 degrees F. Lightly grease broiling tray to prevent sticking and lay chicken pieces on it. Cook 10-12 minutes. Baste with melted ghee or butter or oil. Flip and baste again and cook for another 8-10 minutes. Finally, broil for 3 minutes on each side.

When cooked, place pieces on a flat serving dish. Garnish with slices of onions, wedges of lemon and coriander sprigs.

❦ *TLC Tip: Since this is a time consuming dish, its worth doubling the quantity and freezing some for later use.*

Serving Suggestion
Goes well with rotis or nan, sliced raw onions soaked in lemon juice and cucumber raita.

Preferred kitchenware
- *Medium size frying pan*
- *Broiling tray*
- *4 qt. mixing bowl with lid*
- *Blender*

Tandoori Chicken

A Colorful Spicy Chicken Preparation Traditionally Cooked in Deep Clay Oven Called "Tandoor" with Charcoal

Serves 4

Preparation time: 6 hrs.
Cooking time: 30 mins.

Ingredients:

4 pounds chicken leg quarters or leg pieces, skinned
Marinating (Step 1):
1 teaspoon salt
2 tablespoons lemon juice
Marinating (Step 2):
$1^1/_2$ teaspoons salt
1 teaspoon red chili powder
1 teaspoon coriander powder
1 teaspoon garam masala
4 teaspoons paprika
4 tablespoons ginger paste
3 tablespoons garlic paste
4 tablespoons lemon juice
$^1/_4$ teaspoon red food color
$^1/_4$ teaspoon yellow food color
4 tablespoons oil
$1^1/_2$ cups plain yogurt strained in cheesecloth for 30 minutes

4 oz melted butter or oil for basting
Garnish:
1 tablespoon chat masala*
1 large onion, cut into rings
1 lemon, cut into wedges
4-5 sprigs of coriander leaves

*Available in Indian grocery stores

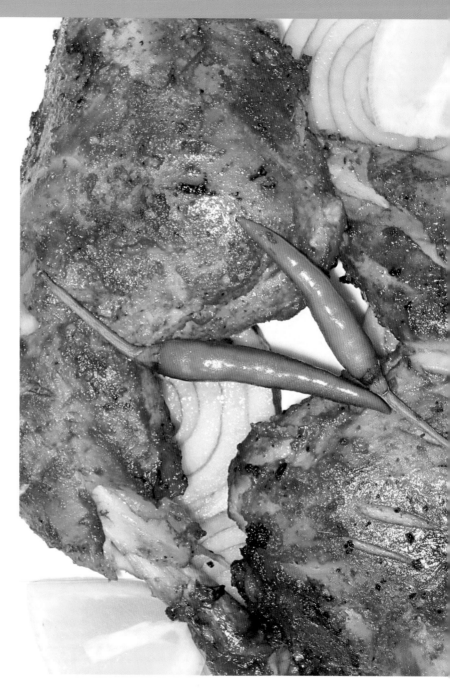

Method:

Marinate - Step 1:
Wash chicken pieces and dry with paper towel. Make deep slits and rub with first step marinating ingredients. Keep aside for 1 hour.

Marinate -Step 2:
In the other bowl add the second marinating step ingredients and mix. Put chicken pieces in this mixture and rub in marinade into slits. Mix and set aside for 4 hours at room temperature or overnight in refrigerator.

Thaw chicken if refrigerated. Preheat oven to 400 degrees F. Lightly grease broiling tray to prevent sticking and lay chicken pieces on it. Cook about 10 minutes. Baste with butter or oil, flip, baste again and cook for another 8-10 minutes. Finally, broil for 3 minutes on each side. Before serving, sprinkle with chat masala and serve with onions and lemon wedges. Decorate with coriander sprigs.

❦TLC Tip: Since this is a time consuming dish, it is worth doubling the quantity and freezing some for later use.

❦TLC Tip: Tandoori chicken is great for barbecuing instead of cooking in oven. Make sure barbecue grill is greased to prevent sticking.

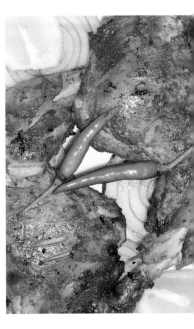

Serving Suggestion
Goes well with tandoori rotis or nan, sliced raw onions soaked in lemon juice and cucumber raita.

Preferred kitchenware
- *Broiling tray*
- *2 - 4 qt. mixing bowls with lids*
- *Cheesecloth*
- *Large strainer*

Goan Fish or Shrimp Curry

Serves 4

Preparation time: 1 hr. 15 mins.
Cooking time: 20 mins.

Ingredients:

$^1/_2$ teaspoon turmeric powder
$1^1/_4$ teaspoons salt
1 lb peeled and washed shrimps or 4 fish fillet cut into 4 inch pieces (catfish preferred)
Spices to be roasted, ground and stored:
2 teaspoons cumin seeds
1 teaspoon mustard seeds
6 teaspoons coriander seeds
1 teaspoon peppercorn
1 teaspoon fenugreek seeds
2 teaspoons chana dal

$2^1/_2$ cups water
1 cup desiccated coconut powder
or $1^1/_2$ cups coconut milk
2 large tomatoes chopped
1 medium green chili
2 cloves of garlic
1 two inch piece ginger
4 tablespoons oil
1 large onion, chopped
$^1/_2$ teaspoon red chili powder
2 tablespoons coriander, chopped

Method:

Rub turmeric powder and salt into shrimps or fish and marinate for 1 hour at room temperature.
Roast the spices to be roasted in frying pan until cumin seeds become light brown. Let cool and grind into fine powder. Keep aside. Add 1 cup boiling water to coconut powder. Let cool and blend to a smooth texture. Squeeze through strainer. (*This is thick milk*). Repeat blending and straining with remaining coconut adding $1^1/_2$ cups cold water. (*This is thin milk*). Keep aside.

Grind tomatoes, green chilies, garlic and ginger.

Heat oil in large saucepan over medium heat, add onions and sauté untill golden brown. Add ground spices, red chili powder, tomatoes, green chili, garlic and ginger mixture and sauté for 2-3 minutes. Add thin milk and let it come to a boil. Add shrimps or fish. Cook covered on low heat for 5 to 7 minutes, stirring occasionally. Turn heat off. Add thick milk. Do not boil. Garnish with chopped coriander.

 TLC Tip: If using coconut milk, dilute $^1/_2$ cup of milk with 1 cup of water for thin milk and undiluted as thick milk.

Serving suggestion
Serve with basmati rice, green vegetables and/or rotis and papad.

Preferred kitchenware
• *4 qt. saucepan (heavy bottomed)*
• *1qt. sauce pan with lid*
• *1 medium frying pan*
• *Large strainer*
• *Blender*
• *Mixing bowl*

Konkan Fried Fish

Serves 4

Preparation time: 2 hrs. 30 mins.
Cooking time: 30 mins.

Ingredients:

1 teaspoon salt
$^1/_4$ teaspoon turmeric powder
$^1/_2$ teaspoon roasted cumin powder
See recipe on page 173
$^1/_2$ teaspoon coriander powder
$1^1/_2$ teaspoons red chili powder
1 tablespoon ginger-garlic paste (or garlic paste)
3 tablespoons lemon juice
4 good-sized filets of Tilapia or Flounder
$^3/_4$ cup semolina
$1^1/_2$ tablespoons rice flour
4 tablespoons oil
For garnish:
Lemon wedges
$^1/_4$ cup coriander sprigs

Method:

Mix salt, turmeric, cumin, coriander, red chili powder, ginger-garlic (or garlic) paste and lemon juice. Rub this mixture into filets. Cover and put in refrigerator for 2 hours to marinate.
Mix semolina and rice flour and put in a zip lock bag. Place 1 marinated filet at a time into the bag and shake until entirely coated.
Heat 2 tablespoons oil in frying pan on medium-high. Lay 2 filets at a time into pan. Reduce heat to medium. When one side is golden brown, turn filet over and brown the other side. Remove from pan and repeat with the other 2 filets. Place filets on flat serving dish, garnish with lemon wedges and coriander sprigs.

Serving suggestion
Serve with brown or white basmati rice and cucumber raita.

Preferred kitchenware
- *Large nonstick frying pan*
- *Small mixing bowl*
- *Large plastic zip lock bags*

Keema Matar

Ground Meat with Peas

Serves 4

Preparation time: 20 mins.
Cooking time: 40 mins.

Ingredients:

3 tablespoons oil
6 pieces black cardamoms
5-6 bay leaves
1 large onion, chopped
1 tablespoon coriander powder
1 tablespoon garlic, finely chopped
2 tablespoons green chili, chopped
1 tablespoon ginger, finely chopped
$1^1/_2$ cups fresh or canned tomatoes, crushed
$1^1/_2$ teaspoons salt
$^1/_2$ teaspoon turmeric powder
$^1/_2$ teaspoon red chili powder
1 cup shelled peas (fresh or frozen)
1 pound lean ground chicken (ground mutton, turkey or lamb can be substituted for chicken)
1 cup water
1 teaspoon garam masala
1 teaspoon paprika (for color)
2 tablespoons coriander, chopped

Serving suggestion
Serve with nan or roti, sliced onions in lemon and salad.

Preferred kitchenware
• *Large nonstick frying pan with lid*

Method:

Heat oil in frying pan over medium heat. Add black cardamoms and bay leaves. Stir. Add onions and stir until they become transparent (about 10-12 minutes). Add coriander powder, garlic, green chilies, ginger, and stir. Add crushed tomatoes and remaining spices, except garam masala and paprika. Stir for 3 to 4 minutes. Add peas, stir, cover, and turn heat to medium-low and cook for about 5 minutes. Add chicken (or one of other meats) and water and bring heat to medium-high. Keep stirring for 10 to 15 minutes or until oil clearly separates from rest of the mixture. Remove from heat, add garam masala and paprika. Cook for another minute. Garnish with chopped coriander and serve hot.

*Picture shown is Lamb Keema.

Lamb or Mutton Curry with Vegetables
Serves 4

Preparation time: 20 mins.
Cooking time: 45 mins.

Ingredients:
$1^1/_2$ pounds lamb or goat (cubed)
4 tablespoons oil
$^1/_2$ teaspoon cumin seeds
2 medium onions, chopped
1 tablespoon garlic, finely chopped
1 teaspoon salt
$^1/_4$ teaspoon turmeric powder
1 teaspoon red chili powder
1 tablespoon coriander powder
$^1/_2$ teaspoon peppercorns
3 medium tomatoes, chopped
1 medium green chili, sliced
1 cup green beans, cut into one inch pieces
2 small carrots, sliced
$1^1/_2$ cups water
$^1/_4$ teaspoon garam masala

Method:
Wash and drain meat. Heat oil in pan over medium-high heat. Add cumin seeds. When seeds start to pop, add onions and garlic. Sauté on medum-high heat for 2 minutes. Add meat. Sauté on medium-high heat for 5 minutes. Add salt and all spices except garam masala. Sauté for 1 minute. Add tomatoes and vegetables and stir well. Add $1^1/_2$ cups water and cover. Cook on high heat until the curry begins to boil. Add garam masala. Turn heat to low and simmer for 25-30 minutes, stirring occasionally.

🍎 *TLC Tip: Save leftovers in an airtight container and freeze. It will taste good later.*

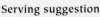

Serving suggestion
Goes well with roti or nan and onions in lemon.

Preferred kitchenware
• *4 qt. heavy bottomed saucepan*

Mutton Chops
Serves 4

Preparation time: 2 hrs. 15 mins.
Cooking time: 35 mins.

Ingredients:

2 pounds mutton chops
1 cup plain yogurt
2 teaspoons ginger-garlic paste (or garlic paste)
1 teaspoon salt
$^1/_2$ teaspoon turmeric powder
4 tablespoons oil
3 black cardamoms
1 two-inch piece of cinnamon stick
3 bay leaves
2 large onions, sliced
2 teaspoons red chili powder
1 cup tomato puree
$1^1/_2$ teaspoons garam masala

Method:

Wash chops thoroughly in running water to remove any 'meaty' odor. Place in strainer to drain.
Marinate: Whisk yogurt and add ginger-garlic (or garlic) paste, salt and turmeric powder. Place chops in marinade for 2 hours.
Heat oil in pan over medium-high heat. Sauté black cardamoms, cinnamon stick and bay leaves for 2 to 3 minutes. Add sliced onions and sauté until light golden brown. Reduce heat to medium. Add chops along with marinade to the onion mixture, stir well, cover and cook until all water has evaporated. When meat is tender, add chili powder and tomato puree. Cook until oil floats to top, indicating that the dish is ready. Add garam masala and stir.

Serving suggestion
Serve with roti or nan with onions in lemon.

Preferred kitchenware
- *Strainer*
- *Large nonstick frying pan*
- *Whisk*

Rogan Josh
Mutton Curry
Serves 4

Preparation time: 1 hr.
Cooking time: 1 hr. 20 mins.

Ingredients:

Masala for roasting
1 teaspoon coriander seeds
1 teaspoon cumin seeds
1 teaspoon poppy seeds
6 whole cloves
6 black cardamoms
12 peppercorns
1 tablespoon coconut, desiccated
1 tablespoon almonds

1 small piece ginger
4 cloves garlic
$1/4$ cup water (for grinding masala)
5 tablespoons ghee or oil
5 green cardamoms
1 large onion, finely chopped
1 teaspoon salt
$1/2$ teaspoon turmeric powder
1 teaspoon red chili powder
$1/6$ teaspoon mace
$1/6$ teaspoon nutmeg
1 cup tomatoes, crushed
4 tablespoons yogurt, beaten
$1^1/_2$ pounds mutton (substitute lamb if preferred)
$1/4$ cup water (for gravy)
$1/2$ teaspoon garam masala
2 tablespoons coriander, chopped

Method:

Roast masalas indicated for roasting in frying pan on medium heat . Keep stirring until the mixture turns brown. Let cool.

Blend ginger, garlic, roasted masalas and $1/4$ cup of water to a fine paste in blender.

Heat oil in saucepan on medium high heat. Sauté green cardamoms and chopped onions till golden brown. Add salt, turmeric powder, red chili powder, mace, nutmeg and masala paste. Turn heat to medium. Stir for 5 minutes. Add crushed tomatoes and cook for 5 minutes. Add yogurt. Cook for 2 to 3 minutes. Add mutton and water, cover, turn heat to low, and simmer for 1 hour or until mutton gets tender. Add garam masala. Garnish with chopped coriander.

Serving suggestion
This dish goes well with nan or tandoori roti and onions in lemon on the side.

Preferred kitchenware
- *4 qt. heavy bottomed saucepan*
- *Blender*
- *Small frying pan*

Frankies
Spicy Meat Rolls
Makes about 10

Preparation time: 30 mins.
Cooking time: 1 hr. 40 mins.

Ingredients:

Meat filling:
2 lbs boneless lamb or goat meat, cut into small cubes
2 medium size onions, chopped
2 green chilies
1 teaspoon cumin seeds
2 tablespoons coriander, chopped
1 one inch piece ginger
2 cloves garlic
3 tablespoons oil
1 teaspoon garam masala
1 teaspoon red chili powder
$^1/_2$ teaspoon salt
$^1/_4$ cup vinegar
Rotis:
6 ounces warm water
2 cups all purpose flour (dough)
$^1/_4$ cup all purpose flour (for rolling)
4 large eggs
1 tablespoon oil
To garnish:
1 medium onion, chopped
2 tablespoons green chilies, finely chopped
2 tablespoons chat masala*

Method:

Meat filling: Wash meat thoroughly in running water, cut into small cubes, and set aside to drain. Grind onions, green chilies, cumin seeds, coriander leaves, ginger and garlic into a fine paste. Heat 3 tablespoons of oil in pan over medium heat and sauté the paste until light brown. Add garam masala, chili powder, salt and meat. Cook for 5 minutes. Add vinegar, cover and cook until meat is tender and liquid is absorbed over medium-low heat.

Rotis: Follow procedure for making rotis as described on page 105. Set rotis aside.

Heat frying pan on medium heat. Beat eggs until fluffy. Place roti over heated pan and put 2 tablespoons of beaten eggs on top of roti. Cook for half a minute, add a little oil and flip roti. Repeat the same for the other side. When the second side is cooked, spread 1 tablespoon of meat and garnish with onions, green chilies and sprinkle with a little chat masala and fold roti to form a roll.

🍃 *TLC Tip: Frozen precooked rotis can be bought from Indian grocery stores.*

Serving suggestion
Serve with green salad.

Preferred kitchenware
- *4 qt. saucepan*   • *Spatula*
- *Medium nonstick frying pan*
For rotis:
- *2 qt. mixing bowl*   • *Tongs*
- *Flour board*   • *Cake cooling rack*
- *Rolling pin*   *(not needed for gas stoves)*

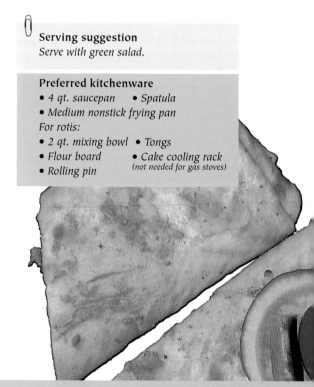

*Available in Indian grocery stores.

Pickles, Raitas, Chutneys and Condiments

Nariyal Lahsan Chutney
Coconut Garlic Chutney
Preparation time: 15 mins.

Ingredients:
1 cup dry unsweetened coconut powder
1 whole bulb of raw garlic
1 teaspoon salt
$^3/_4$ teaspoon red chili powder
1 teaspoon tamarind paste
$^1/_2$ cup water
1 tablespoon oil
1 teaspoon mustard seeds

Method:
Grind all ingredients (*except mustard seeds and oil*) in blender with $^1/_2$ cup of water into a fine paste. Heat oil in frying pan on medium heat and add mustard seeds. When seeds start to pop, remove from pan and add to above mixture.

❦ *TLC Tip: This chutney can be frozen in small containers and thawed when required.*

Serving suggestions
Can be served with idli and sambhar.

Preferred kitchenware
• *Blender*
• *Small frying pan*

Nariyal Chutney
Coconut Chutney
Preparation time: 15 mins.

Ingredients:
$^3/_4$ cup unsweeted dry coconut powder
3 tablespoons roasted chana dal
1 teaspoon salt
$^1/_4$ teaspoon red chili powder
1 medium green chili
$^1/_4$ cup coriander, chopped
2 tablespoons plain yogurt
2 tablespoons lemon juice
$^3/_4$ cup water
For tempering:
2 tablespoons oil
$^1/_4$ teaspoon urad dal
$^3/_4$ teaspoon mustard seeds
4 green curry leaves
2 whole dried red chilies (optional)

Method:
Grind all ingredients (*except those for tempering*) into a fine paste. Place mixture in a bowl and set aside. Heat oil in saucepan on medium-high. Add urad dal and mustard seeds. When seeds start to pop, remove from heat. Add curry leaves and whole red chilies. Add mixture to the chutney and mix.

❦ *TLC Tip: This chutney can be frozen in small containers and thawed when required.*

Serving suggestion
This chutney is usually served with idli and dosa.

Preferred kitchenware
• *Blender*
• *Small frying pan*
• *Medium mixing bowl*

Nimbu Pyaz
Lemon Marinated Onions

Preparation time: 15 mins.
Marination time: 2-3 hrs.

Ingredients:
2 cups onions, thinly sliced
1 teaspoon salt
Juice from 4 large lemons

Method:
Mix ingredients in bowl and marinate at room temperature for a few hours. Store in a glass jar in refrigerator.

❦ *TLC Tip: Use Vidalia onions with a little bit of dried crushed mint flakes and touch of red chili powder for a refreshing side dish in summer.*

Serving suggestion
As a delicious accompaniment to any meat or spicy dish.

Preferred kitchenware
• *Small mixing bowl*

Sirka Pyaz
Red Pearl Onions in Vinegar

Preparation time: 30 mins.
Marination time: 4-6 hrs.

Ingredients:
2 cups red pearl onions, peeled
1 teaspoon salt
$1/2$ cup white vinegar

Method:
Pierce onions with a sharp knife. Mix ingredients in bowl and marinate at room temperature for a few hours. Store in a glass jar in refrigerator.

Serving suggestion
As a delicious accompaniment to any meat or spicy dish.

Preferred kitchenware
• *Small mixing bowl*

Tali Adrak

Shallow Fried Ginger

Preparation time: 10 mins.
Cooking time: 10 mins.

Ingredients:

2 tablespoons oil
$1/_2$ cup ginger, peeled and thinly sliced sticks
$1/_2$ teaspoon salt

Method:

Heat oil in tawa or frying pan over medium heat. Add ginger. Stir till crispy light brown. Remove from heat. Let cool, add salt and stir. Can be stored at room temperature.

Serving suggestion
Goes well with meals containing dals or alu and poori.

Preferred kitchenware
• *Tawa or small frying pan*

Nimbu, Mirch and Adrak

Lemon Marinated Chili or Ginger

Preparation time: 30 mins.
Marination time: 2-3 days

Ingredients:

$1/_2$ cup green chilies, thinly sliced and/or
$1/_2$ cup fresh tender ginger, cut into sticks about 1 inch long and $1/_8$ by $1/_8$ inch thick
$1/_2$ teaspoon salt per half cup
Juice from 2 large lemons per half cup

Method:

Mix ingredients in bowl and marinate at room temperature for a few hours. Chilies will turn yellow and ginger pink. Store in a glass jar in refrigerator.

Serving suggestion
As a delicious accompaniment to any traditional meal.

Preferred kitchenware
• *Small mixing bowl*

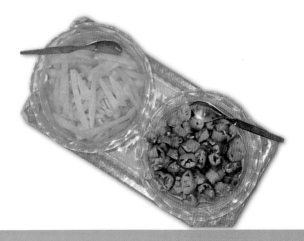

Imli Chutney

Tamarind Chutney

Preparation time: 5 mins.
Cooking time: 10 mins.

Ingredients:

2 tablespoons tamarind paste
$1/2$ cup water
$1/2$ teaspoon salt
$1/8$ teaspoon black salt
$3/4$ teaspoon cumin, roasted and ground
$1/2$ teaspoon red chili powder
$1/2$ teaspoon garam masala
$1/2$ cup sugar

Method:

Mix tamarind paste and water in saucepan and boil over medium heat. Add remaining ingredients. Cook on medium heat for 6 to 7 minutes. Remove from heat and let cool.

 TLC Tip: This chutney can be frozen in a small containers and thawed when required.

Serving suggestion
This chutney is usually served with Chat, Bhel, Dahi Bada, etc.

Preferred kitchenware
• *$1^1/_2$ qt. saucepan*

Dhania and Podina Chutney

Coriander and Mint Chutney

Preparation time: 30 mins.

Ingredients:

1 cup coriander, washed and cleaned
1 cup mint, washed and cleaned
3 tablespoons lemon juice
$1/8$ cup water
1 medium green chili
$1/2$ teaspoon salt
$1/2$ teaspoon cumin seeds
$1/4$ teaspoon red chili powder
Pinch of asafetida

Method:

Purée coriander, mint, lemon juice, water and green chili (a little at a time) into a very fine paste. Add the rest of the ingredients and grind again.

 TLC Tip: This chutney can be frozen in an ice cube tray. Store in freezer bags. Thawed for instant fresh chutney any time.

Serving suggestion
Goes well with meals containing dals.

Preferred kitchenware
• *Blender*

Anannas Lonji

Pickle like Spiced Pineapple Side Dish

Preparation time: 10 mins.
Cooking time: 15 mins.

Ingredients:

1 (20 oz) can unsweetened crushed pineapple
1 tablespoon oil
$1/4$ teaspoon cumin seeds
$1/4$ teaspoon mustard seeds
$1/2$ teaspoon salt
$1/4$ teaspoon turmeric powder
$1/4$ teaspoon red chili powder
$1/2$ teaspoon dry mango powder
$1/2$ teaspoon garam masala
$2 1/2$ teaspoons sugar
1 tablespoon coriander, chopped

Method:

Drain liquid from canned pineapple. Add oil, cumin and mustard seeds to frying pan over medium-high heat. When seeds start to pop, add pineapple, salt and turmeric powder. Cook for 2 to 3 minutes. Add remaining ingredients and stir. Lower heat and cover. Cook for 5 to 7 minutes. Garnish with coriander when cool.

Serving suggestion
Serve as a side dish with meals and snacks.

Preferred kitchenware
• *Medium nonstick frying pan*
• *Large strainer*

Quick Nimbu Achar
Quick Lemon Pickle

Traditional achars take weeks to get ready. This is a quick version.

Preparation time: 10 mins.
Cooking time: 25 mins.

Ingredients:

6 large lemons
$^1/_2$ teaspoon salt
$^1/_2$ teaspoon red chili powder
$^3/_4$ teaspoon garam masala
5 teaspoons sugar

Method:

Wash lemons thoroughly. Cut into halves and again 8 slices per half. Do not peel. Deseed. Put lemon slices into bowl, add salt, chili powder and garam masala. Microwave on high heat for 7 minutes. Stir and microwave for another 5 minutes. Add sugar and mix. Cook another 3 to 4 minutes. Let cool.

🌱 *TLC Tip: Store in a glass jar and refrigerate if used over a period of time.*

Serving suggestion
As an accompaniment to any meal. Goes well with matharis.

Preferred kitchenware
• *2 qt. microwaveable bowl with lid*

Kheera and Other Raitas
Delicately Spiced Yogurt with Vegetables
Serves 4

Preparation time: 15 mins.

Ingredients:

1 cup yogurt
$^1/_4$ cup milk
$^1/_8$ cup water
$^1/_2$ teaspoon salt
$^1/_8$ teaspoon black salt (optional)
$^1/_4$ teaspoon red chili powder
$^1/_4$ teaspoon cumin, roasted and ground
See recipe on page 173
1 cucumber

Method:

Mix yogurt, milk and water in mixing bowl until smooth. Add salt and spices and mix again.
Peel and grate cucumber and squeeze out water. Add grated cucumber to yogurt mixture.

Other varieties of raita:

Substitute any of these for cucumber:
$^1/_4$ cup boondi*, soaked for five minutes, squeezed lightly
$^1/_4$ cup mint, chopped or ground coarsely
$^1/_4$ cup spinach, chopped or ground coarsely
$^1/_4$ cup of finely chopped tomatoes, onions, cucumber and green chilies
$^1/_4$ cup potatoes, boiled, peeled and crushed
$^1/_2$ cup sliced bananas (add $^1/_2$ teaspoon sugar and a $^1/_4$ teaspoon ground cardamom. Do not use red chili powder and cumin).
* *Boondis are 'mini' gram flour (besan) pakodas. Available in Indian grocery stores.*

Serving suggestions
A refreshing side dish with any meal.

Preferred kitchenware
• *1 qt. mixing bowl*
• *Grater*

Special Palak Raita
Delicately Spiced Yogurt with Spinach
Serves 4

Preparation time: 1 hr.
Cooking time: 10 mins.

Ingredients:
Spinach mixture:
1 teaspoon butter or oil
$1/_2$ teaspoon cumin seeds
$1/_2$ cup frozen chopped spinach, thawed
$1/_2$ teaspoon ginger paste (optional)
$1/_2$ teaspoon garlic paste (optional)

1 cup yogurt
$1/_4$ cup milk
$1/_8$ cup water
$1/_2$ teaspoon salt
$1/_8$ teaspoon black salt (optional)
$1/_4$ teaspoon red chili powder
$1/_4$ teaspoon cumin, roasted and ground
See recipe page 173

Method:
Spinach mixture: Heat butter or oil in frying pan over medium heat and add cumin seeds. When seeds begin to pop, add ingredients for the spinach mixture. Sauté for 5 minutes. Let cool.
Raita: Mix yogurt, milk and water in mixing bowl until smooth. Add salt, black salt, red chili powder, roasted cumin powder and the spinach mixture and mix.

Serving suggestions
A refreshing side dish with any meal. Goes specially well with chicken biryani.

Preferred kitchenware
- *1 qt. mixing bowl*
- *Medium frying pan*

Desserts

Alwar Kalakand

Milk Cake from Alwar
Makes 18 pieces

Preparation time: 5 mins.
Cooking time: 20 mins.

Ingredients:

2 tablespoons unsalted butter
15 ounces whole milk ricotta cheese
1 cup sugar
$1^1/_4$ cups powdered milk
1 leaf of silver warak (fine silver foil – optional)

Method:

Heat frying pan on medium heat. Add butter and ricotta cheese. Stir continuously, removing all lumps. Cook for 5 minutes, add sugar and stir for another 2 minutes. Add powdered milk and continue to stir for 2 minutes.

Remove from heat, mix well, and pour into round casserole dish. Cook in casserole dish in microwave oven for 5-6 minutes on high. Check every 1 to 2 minutes, and make sure that mixture does not overflow. The milk cake should be light golden brown when finished. Let cool for about 1 hour.

Remove from dish and cut into about 18 pieces. Optionally, carefully apply the warak face down, on the top surface and remove the backing before cutting.

Serving suggestions
As an anytime snack or as dessert with any meal.

Preferred kitchenware
• *Nonstick frying pan*
• *1 qt. round deep microwaveable casserole dish*

Besan Burfi

North Indian Sweet also called 'Mohan Thal'

Makes about 20 pieces

Preparation time: 10 mins.
Cooking time: 1 hr.

Ingredients:

4 ounces ricotta cheese
$^1/_2$ cup melted ghee
$1^1/_2$ cups gram flour (besan)
Syrup:
$^1/_2$ cup water
1 cup sugar
$^1/_2$ teaspoon ground cardamom
5-6 strands saffron
2-3 drops yellow food coloring (optional)

1 tablespoon raw pistachio, chopped

Method:

Heat frying pan on medium heat. Add ricotta cheese and keep stirring until all liquid has evaporated. Do not brown. Remove from heat and set aside.

Heat large saucepan on low heat. Add ghee and gram flour, stirring continuously until golden brown. Remove pan from stove and add ricotta cheese, combining ingredients until blended. Set aside.

Syrup: Add water and sugar to saucepan and heat on high heat. When mixture starts to boil, reduce heat to medium-low. Add ground cardamom, saffron, food coloring, and cook for 6 to 7 minutes until mixture becomes thick. Turn heat to low and quickly add gram flour mixture to syrup. Stir until mixture releases from sides of pan.

TLC Tip: Do not touch mixture as it will be very hot. Spread mixture 1 inch thick on greased cookie sheet. Sprinkle chopped pistachios and press very lightly. Let cool for approximately 5 to 6 hours and cut into squares.

TLC Tip: Besan burfi can be frozen in air tight containers for future use.

Serving suggestion
As an anytime snack or dessert with any meal.

Preferred kitchenware
- *Large nonstick saucepan*
- *Medium nonstick frying pan*
- *2 qt. saucepan*
- *Cookie sheet, greased*

Besan Ka Halwa

Hot Gram Flour Pudding
Serves 4

Preparation time: 10 mins.
Cooking time: 15 mins.

Ingredients:

1 cup gram flour (besan)
$^1/_2$ cup ghee or unsalted butter, melted
1 $^3/_4$ cups warm water
1 cup sugar
$^1/_2$ teaspoon cardamom, ground
Pinch of saffron, crushed
For garnish:
$^1/_2$ tablespoon raw pistachio, chopped
$^1/_2$ tablespoon almond, chopped

Method:

Add gram flour and ghee to frying pan or kadhai on medium heat. Keep stirring to make sure there are no lumps. Stir until deep golden brown in color (about 5 minutes). Add warm water while stirring and turn heat to low. Add sugar, cardamom, saffron and keep stirring for 1 minute. Turn heat off, cover and let stand for 5 minutes. Add garnish and serve.

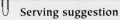

Serving suggestion
A delicious hot pudding usually served with breakfast.

Preferred kitchenware
• *Medium kadhai or frying pan with lid*

Sooji Halwa

Hot Semolina Pudding
Serves 4

Preparation time: 10 mins.
Cooking time: 20 mins.

Ingredients:

1 cup semolina
$^1/_2$ cup ghee
2$^1/_2$ cups warm water
1$^1/_4$ cups sugar
1 teaspoon cardamom, finely ground
Pinch of saffron, crushed
For garnish:
1 tablespoon raw pistachio, chopped
1 tablespoon almond, finely chopped

Method:

Add semolina and ghee to kadhai or frying pan on medium heat. Stir continuously until light brown in color (5-6 minutes). Add warm water while stirring. Add sugar, cardamom, saffron and mix. Let cook on low heat for 2 to 3 minutes stirring all the while. Turn heat off, cover and let stand for 5 minutes. Add garnish and serve.

❧ *TLC Tip: To make halwa a little creamier, replace 1 cup of water with 1 cup of whole milk. Garnishing with raisins and cashews adds a rich taste.*

Serving suggestions
Traditionally eaten with breakfast or a meal with poori. Also used as Prasad (offering) if holding Puja (religious service).

Preferred kitchenware
• *Medium kadhai or frying pan with lid*

Besan Laddoo
Sweet Fragrant Gram Flour Balls
Makes 14

Preparation time: 5 mins.
Cooking time: 1 hr. 30 mins.

Ingredients:

$1^1/_2$ cups gram flour (besan)
$^1/_2$ cup ghee, melted
1 cup sugar
1 teaspoon cardamom, finely ground

Method:

Heat frying pan on medium heat and add gram flour and ghee. Mix both ingredients well and continue stirring until golden brown (about 10 minutes). Remove from heat and let cool for 1 hour (mixture should still be warm). Add sugar and cardamom to warm mixture, and mix well to remove all lumps. Divide the mixture into 14 portions. Take each portion and press into a ball (slightly smaller than a golf ball). Place on a tray and let cool.

Serving suggestion
By itself as a snack or on festive occasions like Diwali.

Preferred kitchenware
• *Medium kadhai or nonstick frying pan*

Choorme ke Laddoo
Sweet Fragrant Flour Balls
Makes 14

Preparation time: 30 mins
Cooking time: 2 hrs

Ingredients:

2 cups whole wheat flour
$^1/_4$ cup melted ghee (for kneading)
4 oz. warm water (for kneading)
2-3 tablespoons oil (for rolling)
2-3 cups oil (for frying)
1 cup sugar
1 teaspoon cardamom, finely ground
10-12 strands saffron, crushed by hand
4 tablespoons melted ghee for making laddoos

Method:

Mix well 2 cups of flour and $^1/_4$ cup of ghee in a medium bowl. Add water and knead until dough does not stick to bowl. (❦ *TLC Tip: It may help to put some oil on your hands to prevent dough from sticking to fingers*). Cover and set aside for 15 minutes.

Knead and divide dough into 6 equal parts. Squeeze each portion between your hands and shape into a ball. Lightly press between palms to flatten to 2 inch diameter. Apply oil very lightly to rolling pin and the flour board. Roll out with rolling pin to approximately 5 inch diameter. (❦ *TLC Tip: Apply a little oil to dough 2 to 3 times to prevent sticking to flour board*)

Heat oil in kadhai over medium heat. (❦ *TLC Tip: To test if oil is hot enough, take a pinch of dough and put in kadhai. It should rise to the surface quickly, if not, wait and try again*). Add 1 rolled out piece of dough (called poori) at a time (❦ *TLC Tip: Slide poori in from side. Do not drop in the middle. Splashed oil can cause serious burns*). It may help the puffing if you keep pressing poori with slotted spoon with very light pressure. When one side has turned light brown, flip and fry the other side. Drain excess oil and remove. When all 6 pooris are done, remove kadhai from stove. After pooris have cooled down to room temperature, break them into small pieces and grind in food processor to as fine a powder as possible (about the size of raw sugar grains).

Add sugar, cardamom, saffron and 4 tablespoons of melted ghee to the powdered pooris, and mix well to remove all lumps. Take a portion of the mixture and press into a ball (about the size of a golf ball). Place on a tray. Alternatively, choorma can be served loose and eaten with a spoon.

❦ *TLC Tip: Choorme ke laddoo can be frozen in air tight containers for future use.*

Serving suggestion
As a snack or with a Bati meal.

Preferred kitchenware
- *2 qt. mixing bowl*
- *Flour board*
- *Rolling pin*
- *Kadhai or deep frying pan*
- *Jharar (slotted spoon)*
- *Food processor*
- *Large mixing bowl*

Fruit Cream
Light Fresh Fruit Dessert
Serves 4

Preparation time: 15 mins.

Ingredients:
$^1/_2$ pint heavy or light cream
3 tablespoons sugar
1 banana, thinly sliced
$^1/_2$ apple, peeled and cut into small cubes
$^1/_4$ cup grapes, cut in half
$^1/_4$ cup strawberries, sliced
1 small can fruit cocktail, drained
1 small can Mandarin oranges, drained
(other fruits such as pineapple, mango, etc.
can also be added)

Method:
Mix cream and sugar in bowl. Add fruits and
mix lightly. Serve chilled.

Serving suggestions
*Serve in glass bowls as a refreshing and
light dessert.*

Preferred kitchenware
• *2 qt. mixing bowl*

Gulab Jamun

Fragrant Milk Balls in Light Syrup
Makes about 25

Preparation time: 20 mins.
Cooking time: 45 mins.
Soaking time: 4 hrs.

Ingredients:

1 cup self rising flour
1 cup powdered milk (Carnation brand preferred)
$^1/_2$ pint heavy cream
2 cups oil (for frying)
For syrup:
6 cups water
4 cups sugar
$^1/_4$ teaspoon saffron

Method:

Mix flour, powdered milk and cream. Knead into dough. Let stand 10 minutes. Grease hands lightly with oil. Smooth dough, removing all dents on the surface. Divide into 25 equal parts. Using both palms, mold each into a ball. Heat oil in kadhai over medium heat.

 TLC Tip: To test temperature of oil put a small drop of dough in; if it rises to the surface rapidly, it is ready. If it stays at the bottom or rises very slowly, wait and try again. Remove the test piece from oil before starting to fry.

Add 10 balls at a time and fry until dark brown in color, turning constantly. Remove and set aside.

Syrup: Add water and sugar to saucepan placed on high heat. When mixture starts to boil, reduce heat to medium. Add saffron and cook for 25 minutes until mixture reaches the consistency of light syrup. Remove from heat. Add balls to syrup and cover for 3 to 4 hours, until they become saturated with syrup. Serve warm or cold.

TLC Tip: Gulab Jamun can be frozen in air tight containers for future use.

Serving suggestion
Serve warm or chilled as an anytime snack or as dessert. Also for festive occasions like Diwali.

Preferred kitchenware
- *Medium kadhai or deep frying pan*
- *6 qt. saucepan*
- *2 qt. mixing bowl*
- *Slotted spoon*

Kheer
Indian Style Rice Pudding
Serves 4

Preparation time: 30 mins.
Cooking time: 2 hrs.

Ingredients:

5 cups milk
$1/_4$ cup basmati rice
$1/_4$ pint light cream
$1/_3$ cup sugar
7 pieces of almond, soaked, peeled and sliced
Pinch of saffron, crushed
1/2 teaspoon cardamom, ground
For garnish:
1 tablespoon raw pistachio, finely chopped

Method:

Boil milk over medium heat, stirring occasionally to prevent scorching the bottom of saucepan. Add rice and cream and reduce heat to low. Cook for $1^1/_2$ hours, stirring occasionally. Add sugar and cook for another 5 minutes. Remove from heat. Add almonds, saffron and cardamom. Garnish with pistachio. Serve warm or chilled.

Serving suggestion
Whether warm or chilled, this delicious rice pudding complements any meal.

Preferred kitchenware
• *3 qt. saucepan*

Mango Ice Cream
Serves 4

Preparation time: 15 mins.
Freezing time: 12 hrs.

Ingredients:

15 ounces fresh or canned mango pulp
8 ounces Cool Whip or other whipped cream
14 ounces condensed milk
1 fresh mango, peeled and cut into small cubes for topping (optional)

Method:

Combine all ingredients (except fresh mango for topping) and freeze mixture (takes about a day). Cut into square pieces and serve topped with fresh mango.
❦ *TLC Tip: Can be stored up to two months in freezer in an airtight container.*

Serving suggestion
Delicious finish to any meal or as a refreshing dessert.

Preferred kitchenware
• *Rectangular plastic container with lid*

Nan Khatai

Indian Style Butter Cookies

Makes about 20

Preparation time: 15 mins.
Cooking time: 30 mins.

Ingredients:

$1^1/_4$ cups all purpose flour
4 tablespoons sugar
1 stick melted unsalted butter
2 tablespoons raw pistachio, finely chopped

Method:

Mix ingredients except pistachio in mixing bowl into a soft dough. Do not knead. Divide into 20 equal portions. Make each portion into a ball then gently press to flatten slightly. Sprinkle pistachio nuts over middle of each ball. Arrange on cookie sheet, leaving room between balls.

Preheat oven to 350°F. Place cookie sheet on the middle rack and bake for 20 minutes or until golden brown.

Serving suggestions
Tastes great with milk or tea.

Preferred kitchenware
• *2 qt. mixing bowl*
• *Rectangular nonstick cookie sheet*

Peda

Sweet Milk Patties

Makes 24 pieces

Preparation time: 15 mins.
Cooking & setting time: 12 hrs.

Ingredients:

$^3/_4$ stick unsalted butter
$^3/_4$ cup milk
$^3/_4$ cup sugar
$2^1/_2$ cups nonfat dry milk (Carnation brand preferred)
For garnish:
2 tablespoons raw pistachio, finely chopped

Method:

Heat saucepan over medium heat. Add butter, milk and sugar. Keep stirring until mixture boils. Add powdered milk. Keep stirring for 10 minutes, until it thickens. Remove from heat and let cool.

Divide into 24 pieces. Make into balls and flatten between palms to $1^1/_2$ inch diameter. Molds can also be used for a fancy look. Create a dimple in the middle of ball with finger, and add garnish. Let solidify overnight.

Serving suggestion
As a delicious snack or for festive occasions such as Diwali.

Preferred kitchenware
• *4 qt. saucepan*

Ras Malai
Cheese Balls in Light Cream Sauce
Makes 20

Preparation time: 10 mins.
Cooking time: 6 hrs.

Ingredients:
$^1/_2$ gallon 2 percent fat milk
4 tablespoons white vinegar
$4^1/_2$ cups water
$1^1/_2$ cups sugar
2 tablespoons rose water*
Cream:
1 cup whole milk
1 quart half and half
$^1/_4$ cup sugar
To garnish:
1 tablespoon raw pistachio, finely chopped
7-8 strands saffron, crushed
*Available in Indian grocery stores.

Method:
Bring milk to boil over medium heat stirring occasionally to prevent scorching at the bottom. Add vinegar to curdle milk and remove from heat. Strain curdled milk in cheesecloth (draped over strainer) over the sink to separate whey from solid portion. Set aside for 3 hours. Blend drained solids in food processor to a fine mixture. Make 20 equal-sized balls, flatten slightly.

Boil water on high heat. Add sugar. Wait till sugar dissolves. Add cheese balls and cover for 5 minutes. Balls should now be double in size. Reduce heat to medium, cover and cook for another 15 minutes. Turn off heat and add rose water. Let cool. Remove balls and squeeze out syrup gently with hands. Set aside.

Boil milk with half and half, over medium heat. Reduce heat to medium-low and let cook for about 45 minutes stirring occasionaly, until it reaches the consistency of light cream. Add sugar and cook for another 2 minutes. Remove from heat, add balls, let cool and garnish.

Serving suggestion
Serve chilled as a party dessert.

Preferred kitchenware
- *6 qt. saucepan*
- *3 qt. saucepan*
- *Cheesecloth*
- *Large strainer*
- *Food processor*

Rasgulla
Cheese Balls in Light Syrup from Bengal
Makes 20

Preparation time: 10 mins.
Cooking time: 5 hrs.

Ingredients:
$^1/_2$ gallon 2 percent fat milk
4 tablespoons white vinegar
$4^1/_2$ cups water
$1^1/_2$ cups sugar
2 tablespoons rose water*
For Garnish:
1 tablespoon raw pistachio, sliced (optional)
*Available in Indian grocery stores.

Serving suggestion
Serve chilled as a classy dessert.

Preferred kitchenware
• 6qt. saucepan
• Large strainer
• Food processor
• Cheesecloth

Method:
Boil milk over medium heat stirring occasionally to prevent scorching the bottom of pan. Add vinegar to curdle milk. Remove from heat. Strain curdled milk in cheesecloth placed in strainer over the sink to separate whey from solid portion. Set aside for 3 hours.

Blend drained solids in food processor to a fine mixture. Make 20 equal balls.

Boil water on high heat. Add sugar. wait till sugar dissolves. Add balls and cover for 5 minutes. The balls should now be double in size. Reduce heat to medium, cover and cook an additional 15 minutes. Turn off heat and add rose water. Let cool. Garnish with pistachio slices before serving. (Optional).

Ricotta Burfi

Rectangular Fragrant Sweet Pastries
Makes about 22 pieces

Preparation time: 15 mins.
Cooking and setting time: 12 hrs.

Ingredients:

2 tablespoons unsalted butter
15 ounces whole milk ricotta cheese
$^3/_4$ cup sugar
$^1/_2$ cup blanched almonds, ground
$^3/_4$ cup powdered milk (Carnation brand preferred)
For garnish:
Warak (silver foil-optional) or
$^1/_2$ teaspoon raw pistachio, finely chopped

Method:

Heat frying pan over medium heat. Add butter and
ricotta cheese. Stir for 5 minutes. Add sugar, stir for
4 minutes. Add ground almonds and powdered milk
and stir until mixture becomes like soft dough.
Remove from heat.

Grease cookie sheet. Transfer mixture on the center
of cookie sheet and pat with hands to spread into
$^1/_2$ inch thick layer. Spread warak over entire surface,
removing backing as you go along. Alternatively,
spread chopped pistachio evenly and press lightly.
Let solidify overnight. Cut into $1^1/_2$ inch squares and
serve.

Serving suggestion
*A tasty finish to any meal or a snack by
itself.*

Preferred kitchenware
• *Large nonstick frying pan*
• *Rectangular cookie sheet*

Sevain Kheer

Indian Style Vermicelli Pudding

Serves 4

Preparation time: 15 mins.
Cooking time: 30 mins.

Ingredients:

5 cups whole milk
1 cup roasted Indian vermicelli*, broken into about
2 inch pieces
$^1/_3$ cup sugar
Pinch of saffron, crushed
$^1/_2$ teaspoon cardamom, ground
For garnish:
1 teaspoon raw pistachio, finely chopped
Available in Indian grocery stores

Method:

Boil milk over medium heat stirring occasionally to prevent scorching the bottom. Add vermicelli and reduce heat to low. Stir occasionally and cook for 15-20 minutes. Add sugar and cook for another 5 minutes. Turn heat off. Add saffron and cardamom. Serve warm or chilled. Garnish with pistachio.

Serving suggestion
Traditionally eaten around Raksha Bandhan day in India. Surprise your brothers and guests next Rakhi!

Preferred kitchenware
• *3 qt. heavy bottom saucepan*

Sri Khand

Light Fragrant Yogurt Dessert from
Maharashtra

Serves 4

Preparation time: 5 hrs.

Ingredients:

8 cups plain whole milk yogurt
8 tablespoons sugar
$^1/_2$ teaspoon cardamom, ground
10 strands saffron, crushed
For garnish:
1 teaspoon raw pistachio, chopped
1 teaspoon almond, chopped

Serving suggestion
*Light dessert that can be eaten by itself
or at the end of a meal.*

Preferred kitchenware
• *Cheesecloth*
• *Large strainer*
• *Bowl, large enough for strainer*
• *2 qt. mixing bowl*

Method:

Spread cheesecloth over strainer and place in bowl.
Pour yogurt over cheesecloth and tie edges to prevent
yogurt from spilling out of its sides. Let stand for 3-4
hours until water has drained from yogurt.
Mix yogurt with all ingredients except garnish. Add
garnish and serve chilled.

Drinks

Mango Lassi

Refreshing Mango Yogurt Drink from the Punjab
Serves 4

Preparation time: 15 mins.

Ingredients:

$1^1/_2$ cups fresh or canned mango pulp
2 cups plain yogurt
$^1/_2$ cup milk
6 tablespoons sugar
1 cup ice, crushed

Method:

Blend all ingredients except ice in blender until smooth. Add crushed ice and serve in tall glasses. Spoon out foam from blender on to top of lassi in glass.

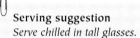

Serving suggestion
Serve chilled in tall glasses.

Preferred kitchenware
• *Blender*

Lassi

Refreshing Yogurt Drink from the Punjab
Serves 4

Preparation time: 10 mins.

Ingredients:

$2 ^1/_2$ cups plain yogurt
1 cup milk
6 tablespoons sugar
2 tablespoons rose water
1 cup ice, crushed

Method:

Blend all ingredients except ice in blender until smooth. Add crushed ice and serve in tall glasses. Spoon out foam from blender on to top of lassi in glass.

Serving suggestion
Serve chilled in tall glasses.

Preferred kitchenware
• *Blender*

Namkeen Lassi

Refreshing Salty Yogurt Drink from the Punjab

Serves 4

Preparation time: 10 mins.

Ingredients:

3 cups plain yogurt
1/2 cup water
1 1/4 teaspoons salt
1/2 teaspoon red chili powder
3/4 teaspoon cumin powder, roasted
See recipe page 173
1 cup ice, crushed

Method:

Blend all ingredients except ice in blender until smooth. Add crushed ice and serve in tall glasses. Spoon out foam from blender on to top of the lassi in the glass.

Serving suggestion
Serve chilled in tall glasses. Goes well with makki ki roti and sag.

Preferred kitchenware
• *Blender*

Masala Adrak Chai

Spicy Tea with Ginger

Serves 4

Preparation time: 15 mins.

Ingredients:

4 pods of green cardamom
4 whole cloves
6-7 strands of saffron
1 one inch stick or pinch of powdered cinnamon
3 $\frac{1}{4}$ cups water
1 one inch piece of ginger, peeled and grated
4 heaping teaspoons loose tea, or 4 tea bags
1 cup 2 percent or whole milk
6 teaspoons sugar or to taste

Method:

Crush spices in mortar to coarse powder (including cardamom skin).

☙*TLC Tip: If you do not have a mortar and pestle, ground spices can be substituted.*

Boil water, spices and ginger in the saucepan over high heat. Add tea, milk and suger and bring to a boil again. Remove from heat and cover. Let stand for 1 to 2 minutes. If using teabags, release additional liquid from teabags by squeezing them against a spoon. Strain and serve.

☙*TLC Tip: Remove label from teabags and tie strings together for easy removal.*

Serving suggestion
Traditional tea with milk. Great anytime of day or as a perfect finish to dinner.

Preferred kitchenware
• *2 qt. saucepan with lid*
• *Mortar and pestle*

Panna

Sweet and Sour Green Mango Drink

Serves 4

Preparation time: 1 hr. 30 mins.

Ingredients:

2 large green mangoes
2 cups water
1 $\frac{1}{2}$ teaspoons salt
$\frac{1}{4}$ teaspoon red chili powder
$\frac{1}{4}$ teaspoon cumin powder, roasted
See recipe page 173
2 $\frac{1}{2}$ tablespoons sugar

Method:

Boil mangoes on medium heat in covered saucepan with enough water to cover them for 45 minutes or until skin gets soft.
Let cool for about 30 minutes.
Peel and scoop out pulp from skin and seeds. Grind pulp with 2 cups water in blender until smooth. Add other ingredients and blend.
Let cool and serve with ice cubes.

🍃*TLC tip: Panna can be used as a delicious side dish with paranthas. In this case use only 1 cup of water and no ice.*

Serving suggestion:
Serve with ice cubes in tall glasses as a refreshing drink on a hot summer day.

Preferred Kitchenware:
• *2 qt. Saucepan with cover*
• *2 qt. Mixing bowl*
• *Blender*

Thandai

Delicious Iced Almond and Herbs Milk
Drink from North India

Serves 4

Preparation time: 30 mins.

Ingredients:

$^3/_4$ cup almonds
$1^1/_2$ teaspoons peppercorns (or to taste)
4 tablespoons fennel seeds
2 teaspoons dried cantaloupe seeds (if available)
$^1/_8$ cup dried rose petals (if available)
2 cups water
3 cups whole milk
$^3/_4$ cup sugar (or to taste)
4-6 drops rose essence*
Crushed ice (as needed)

*Available in Indian grocery stores

Method:

Grind all ingredients (except sugar, milk, ice and rose essence) in blender on high speed with $1^1/_2$ cups water into a paste. Strain into bowl using cheesecloth over strainer with half the milk. Take remaining paste from strainer and put back into blender. Add remaining water and grind again. Strain again with the other half of milk.
Add sugar and stir until completely dissolved.
Add rose essence drops and stir. Add ice and serve.

Serving suggestion
Serve in pitcher with crushed ice in tall glasses. Traditionally served at "Holi" time.

Preferred kitchenware
- *Blender*
- *Cheesecloth*
- *4 qt. mixing bowl*
- *Strainer*

Miscellaneous

INGREDIENTS THAT CAN BE COOKED IN ADVANCE

Ghee
Clarified Butter

Preparation time: 5 mins.
Cooking time: 15 mins.

Ingredients:
4 sticks unsalted butter

Method:
Place butter in saucepan over medium-high heat. When it comes to a boil, reduce heat to medium-low. Cook for 10-12 minutes until the butter becomes clarified. Let cool. Strain and pour into glass bottle.

🍃 *TLC Tip: Can be stored at room temperature for up to fifteen days. Store in the refrigerator for longer duration.*

Preferred kitchenware
- *1 qt. saucepan*
- *Cheesecloth*

Dahi
Home Made Yogurt

Cooking and setting time: 8 hrs.

Ingredients:
3 cups two percent fat or whole milk
1 tablespoon fresh yogurt as culture

Method:
Place milk in saucepan over medium-high heat. Keep stirring frequently to prevent burning at the bottom and let it come to a boil. Cool until luke warm (110-115 deg F - takes about 45 minutes). Mix in yogurt culture. Cover and put in oven with the light on for 6 to 7 hours until it feels firm. Refrigerate before using.

🍲 *TLC Tip: The milk can be boiled in the microwave (8-10 minutes) directly in bowl.*

Preferred kitchenware
- *1 qt. heavy bottom saucepan*
- *Medium microwaveable glass bowl with lid*
- *Meat or other thermometer capable of measuring 110-120 deg F (optional)*

Paneer

Homemade Cheese

Preparation time: 5 mins.
Cooking time: 1 hr.
Setting time: 2 hrs.

Ingredients:

1 gallon whole milk
$^{1}/_{4}$ cup lemon juice
2 cups oil for frying

Method:

Bring milk to boil in saucepan on medium heat, stirring occasionally to prevent burning at the bottom. Turn off heat and immediately add lemon juice.

Place saucepan on low heat again until milk has curdled and separated from whey. Remove from heat and let mixture sit for a few minutes.

Spread cheesecloth over large strainer or colander and pour curdled milk into it. Gather the cheesecloth around the curdled milk and squeeze out excess whey.

❦ *TLC Tip: To get a compact brick of paneer, place a heavy weight, such as a pot filled with water over cheese cloth containing curdled milk for about 2 hours.*

Remove from cheesecloth and cut paneer into 1 inch cubes.

❦*TLC Tip: Deep fry cubes in small kadhai or frying pan on medium heat until light brown. The cubes should remain soft on inside. Set aside to cool. When cooled, store in zip lock bags and freeze. They will be ready the next time you want to make paneer dish.*

❗ Caution: Use extreme care when deep frying. Due to a combination of factors, the object being fried may burst causing the hot oil to spatter. Some of the causes can be adding too much water, the oil being too hot, or the ingredients being old stock due to poor turnover in the store. It is always advisable to stand a fair distance away from the stove until you have made sure this is not happening. Also, you can hold a spatter screen as a safe guard.

Preferred kitchenware
- *Cheesecloth*
- *Large colander or strainer*
- *Large saucepan*
- *Kadhai or deep frying pan*
- *Slotted spoon*

Precooked Masala

Makes about 3 cups

Preparation time: 30 mins.
Cooking time: 1 hr.

Ingredients:
2 medium onions, peeled and sliced
1 large or 2 medium green chilies
2 cloves garlic
2 small pieces of ginger
$1/_2$ cup oil
$1/_2$ teaspoon cumin seeds
4 bay leaves
1 cinnamon stick
4 black cardamoms
28 ounces canned tomatoes, crushed
$1/_2$ teaspoon salt
$1/_2$ teaspoon turmeric powder
$1/_2$ teaspoon red chili powder
4 teaspoons coriander powder
$1/_2$ teaspoon garam masala
$1/_2$ teaspoon paprika (for color)

Method:
Grind onions, green chilies, garlic and ginger in food processor to a fine paste. Heat oil in saucepan over medium-high heat. Add cumin seeds, bay leaves, cinnamon stick and black cardamoms. When cumin seeds start to pop, add onion paste. Lower heat to medium-low and stir occasionally until onions turn golden brown (about 20 minutes).
Meanwhile, purée tomatoes in food processor.
Add rest of the spices and puréed tomatoes to onions. Stir. Turn heat to low. Cover and let cook for 40-45 minutes, stirring occasionally. When oil separates from rest of the sauce, the masala is done.
💐 *TLC Tip: Since this masala takes time to prepare, make a large quantity and freeze in small containers. Remove containers and defrost as needed.*

Preferred kitchenware
• *Food processor*
• *4 qt. nonstick saucepan with lid*

Bhuna Jeera

Roasted and Ground Cumin

Cooking time: 30 mins.

Ingredients:

$^1/_2$ cup cumin seeds

Method:

Heat frying pan over medium heat. Add cumin seeds, stirring until dark brown (2 to 3 minutes). Remove from heat. Wait until seeds cool and grind into a coarse powder in coffee grinder.

❦*TLC Tip: Store in an airtight glass jar at room temperature.*

Preferred kitchenware
- *Small frying pan*
- *Coffee grinder*

Anardana

Roasted Pomegranate Seed Powder

Cooking time: 30 mins.

Ingredients:

1 cup dried pomegranate seeds

Method:

Heat frying pan over medium heat. Add seeds, stirring until dark brown (2 to 3 minutes). Remove from heat. Wait until seeds cool and grind into a fine powder in coffee grinder. Strain into bowl and throw away the remaining.

❦*TLC Tip: Store in an airtight glass jar at room temperature.*

Preferred kitchenware
- *Small frying pan*
- *Coffee grinder*
- *Large strainer*
- *Medium mixing bowl*

Garam Masala
North Indian Spice Blend

Preparation time: 30 mins.

Ingredients:
$^3/_8$ cup black cardamom
$^1/_4$ cup cumin seeds
$^1/_4$ cup cinnamon sticks, broken into 1-2 inch pieces
$^3/_8$ cup peppercorn
$^3/_8$ cup cloves
1 teaspoon green cardamom seeds
3 teaspoons ginger powder
2 cups bay leaves

Method:
Remove the black cardamom seeds from the shells and throw away the shells.
Combine all ingredients and grind into a fine powder in coffee grinder.

❦ *TLC Tip: Store in an airtight glass jar at room temperature.*

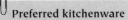

Preferred kitchenware
• *Coffee grinder*

Sambhar Powder
South Indian Spice Blend Used in Sambhar

Preparation Time: 1 hr.

Ingredients:
$1/4$ cup arhar dal
$1/4$ cup chana dal
$1/4$ cup urad dal
1 cup whole red dried chilies
$1^1/4$ cups coriander seeds
$1/8$ cup peppercorn
$1/2$ teaspoon fenugreek seeds

Method:
Heat frying pan over medium heat. Add all the ingredients. Roast for about 10 minutes while stirring. Remove from heat. Wait until spices cool down and grind into a fine powder in coffee grinder.

❦ *TLC Tip: Store in an airtight glass jar at room temperature.*

Preferred kitchenware
- *Medium frying pan*
- *Coffee grinder*

Saunf

Roasted Fennel Seeds with Coconut – an after
Dinner Mouth Freshener

Preparation time: 5 mins.
Cooking time: 30 mins.

Ingredients:

1 cup fennel seeds
$^1/_4$ cup dried sweetened coconut flakes

Method:

Heat frying pan over medium heat and add fennel
seeds. Keep stirring until they turn light golden brown
(2 to 3 minutes). Remove from heat. Allow to cool.
Add coconut flakes and mix well.

❦*TLC Tip: Store in an airtight glass jar at room temperature.*
❦*TLC Tip: In addition to being a mouth freshener, this
mixture has good digestive properties.*

Serving suggestion
*Serve in a small bowl at the end of a
meal with a small spoon.*

Preferred kitchenware
• *Small nonstick frying pan*

More TLC Tips

🍂 More TLC Tips

Here are a few tricks that I have gathered from years of experience that you may find useful. I have classified them into various categories for handy reference.

SAFETY:

• Keep a box of baking soda handy. In case of a minor fire, covering the source of flame with the baking soda will quickly extinguish the fire.

• Always keep a small fire extinguisher within ready reach in or near your kitchen. Everybody in the house should know the location and proper way to use this extinguisher. Occasionally check to make sure it is charged.

• Never leave a kadhai with oil unattended on the stove – not even to answer a phone call. Many house fires have started from the cook being in a phone conversation and completely forgetting about the kadhai.

COOKING CRISIS:

• Use some breadcrumbs to thicken sauce that has become too watery. If out of bread crumbs, toast a slice of bread, let cool and crumble.

• If a dish is too salty, cook some peeled potatoes in the gravy to absorb some of the excess salt. Remove the potatoes before serving.

• If the food burns on the bottom of a pan, transfer contents immediately to a new pan and discard the burned layer. In most cases this will prevent a burnt smell in the food.

PROVEN HOUSEHOLD MEDICATIONS:

• For immediate relief of severe cough or congestion, stir one eighth of a teaspoon of turmeric in a quarter cup of hot milk and drink a few times during the day.

• Put a teaspoon of honey and a little lemon juice in half cup of hot water and drink for immediate relief of sore throats and coughs.

• Make a paste of hing (asafetida) and water and apply a little around the belly button of a baby for immediate relief from gas pain.

• Lightly boil some fennel seeds in water, strain, cool and give to baby for indigestion.

• Have some ginger tea (recipe in the book) for relief from symptoms of cold and flu.

• Eat some mashed ripe banana in plain yogurt for relief from upset stomachs. When recovering from an upset stomach, plain yogurt with khichdi (recipe in the book) is an excellent and light meal.

FRUITS AND VEGETABLES:

- Squeeze the very last drop of juice from a lime or lemon by microwaving it for a few seconds before cutting and squeezing.
- Prevent potatoes and eggplants from turning dark by cutting them in cold water.
- Before peeling a coconut, hit lightly all over with a hammer to separate shell from the fruit.
- Turn soft tomatoes into firm ones by soaking them in cold water with a little salt for a few hours.
- Soak onions in cold water for one half hour before peeling and cutting to prevent eyes from watering.
- For faster ripening of fruits such as mangos and papayas, store in brown paper bags or wrap them in newspapers for a few days before washing.
- If you have extra ripened bananas, peel and wrap individually in plastic film and store in the freezer. Thaw for about ten seconds each in the microwave and use for items such as muffins and banana breads.
- Prevent okras from becoming sticky by making sure they are completely dry before cutting them.

CLEANING AND ODOR REMOVAL:

- Polish silver and diamonds using common toothpastes.
- Clean grease from clothing and carpets by sprinkling the soiled spot with talcum powder. Let stand and wash or remove with a damp cloth.
- Clean wine spills from carpets by applying a little club soda and dabbing off with a paper or cloth towel.
- Clean burned tawas or kadhais by heating and spraying with oven cleaner. Let stand for two hours and scrub clean.
- Remove odors from garbage disposal by grinding half a lemon through the disposal.
- Improve the efficiency of garbage disposal by grinding some crushed ice through it.
- Keep an opened pack of baking soda in the back of the fridge to continuously remove odors.
- Remove odors from cutting boards by rubbing with a little lemon or lime.
- Remove odors from jars by filling with water and a teaspoon of baking soda. Shake and let stand for an hour. Wash thoroughly.
- Cluttered drawers? Try organizing one drawer a day instead of taking the whole task on all at once.

STORING:

- When storing food in freezer, use multiple small bags or containers rather than one large one. This way you will thaw only what you need for one meal.

- The same applies for precooked masalas (recipe in the book).

- Mark bags with permanent ink marker with contents and date stored. When frozen, sometimes it is hard to recognize their contents.

- Freeze chutneys in an ice tray and remove and thaw only the number of cubes you need for a meal.

EVERYDAY AND PARTY COOKING:

- A lot of recipes in the book can be fully or partially cooked in advance to shorten the time required for cooking on the day of the party. These frozen items can also be used to provide a complete and satisfying instantaneous meal for surprise company.

- Get the cooking for the day done and out of the way before embarking on other projects such as shopping or visiting friends. You will be lot more relaxed.

- Once the menu for a party is decided, write down the ingredients needed for each dish to avoid last minute stress and running around.

- Create a list of tasks by day a few days ahead of a party or other entertaining event. This includes:

  - Cooking ahead and freezing what you can. As an example, if making kofta curry, the koftas can be made ahead of time and frozen and cooked with sauce the day of the party.

  - Shopping for items such as drinks and paper products.

  - Any cleaning that can be done in advance.

INDEX - ENGLISH EQUIVALENTS

(v) Vegan or Vegan Option

(v) Vegan or Vegan Option

INDEX - INDIAN NAMES